Your Wake Up Call

Signposts to Sustainability

Published in the United Kingdom in 2006 by
The Community Press
6 Albert Road, Altrincham, Cheshire,
WA15 9AN, England

British Library Cataloguing in Publication Data

ISBN 0-9554580-0-5
      978-0-9554580-0-2

Printed and bound in Great Britain by Lightning Source UK Ltd

Your Wake Up Call

Signposts to Sustainability

Chris Wright

The Community Press

Contents

Introduction

In 1791, Thomas Paine presented what he termed "a small Treatise" to the first President of the United States, George Washington. *The Rights of Man*[1] is a passionate defence of democracy and the principles on which the fledgling Republic had been so recently founded. That he felt the need to rally his fellow citizens shows how much he feared for Freedom in a hostile world.

Two hundred years on and Freedom remains on the critical list, not just across the broad sweep of a world that has never been wholly convinced of its merits, but in the very heartlands of the West itself. Worse still, humanity faces its greatest challenge yet – the real possibility that our collective activities will irreparably harm the planet on which we all depend for life. If only for the sake of our children, we must pause and consider what we are doing. That is the hallmark of a Free people. We *can* choose to do things differently.

And yet, the very decision-making processes that we believe to be the guarantors of our Freedoms are pushing us inexorably and ever faster in a direction that is unsustainable. It is as if we were sleepwalking into the future, fully aware that we are heading for a precipice, but quite unable to stop.

That has been the fate of all previous civilisations that have failed to rise to the challenges that face them. If we truly believe in the power of Freedom to enable us to live securely and sustainably on this crowded planet, we must ask some fundamental questions about what it means to be Free ...

1
Setting the Scene

At any other time in human history the catalogue of greed, exploitation, poverty, disease, war, terror and destruction that passes for news today would have appeared unremarkable. The rich continue to get richer and the poor die younger. The powerful seek to protect and extend their interests, and think nothing of consigning their weaker fellow creatures to death in doing so. And the threat and use of force is never far away. So what's new?

Only in terms of the sheer number of people affected might an eyebrow be raised, but then there are over six billion people alive today (world population reached one billion in the middle of the nineteenth century and was less than half that size three hundred and fifty years earlier in 1500). Population on the scale we see today is a very recent phenomenon. In almost every other respect, however, it is business as usual. Apologists continue to wring their hands and say it is in the nature of the human condition, or a necessary precondition for inevitable improvement at some unspecified time in the future. Critics offer explanations in terms the corruption of absolute power, the conflicting interests of classes, or divine wrath, and prescribe – usually violent –

remedies that, if only followed, will usher in heaven on earth. Meanwhile the seasons pass and little changes.

Faced with the realities of having to get by in this life, only hope has sustained the majority through the ages, hope that tomorrow is another day and things might get better, if not for themselves then for their children. There's always hope in children. What *is* different about the situation today, however, is that, for the first time, we face the very real possibility that there may not be too many tomorrows. The Middle Ages feared the end of the world through cosmic, supernatural intervention: we must grapple with the prospect of an end to our species brought about entirely by our own activities; and, if that happens, we will go out with a whimper rather than a bang, a slow, protracted death on an increasingly hostile planet floating in an endless void ...

The possibility that we ourselves might foul and completely destroy our own habitat has only registered on human consciousness since the Second World War with those images from space of our impossibly beautiful and vulnerable planet, and through the madness of Mutually Assured Destruction. The threat of a nuclear Armageddon hasn't entirely receded but, through luck rather than judgement, we have managed to create an uneasy balance in which the possibility is much reduced. Now our unbridled pursuit of economic growth as an end in itself is creating another set of circumstances that is calling into question our very survival as a species. The challenges we face may not be as obvious as those posed by the proliferation of nuclear weapons. Their nature and extent may still be disputed, but they are coming into ever-sharper focus with each passing day.

- **Global warming and unpredictable climate change:** at the very least, future generations will have to contend with unpredictable periods of severe weather, dwarfing existing hurricanes and tornados in both frequency and force.

- **Resource depletion (especially oil) and environmental degradation:** at the very least, future generations will have to contend with significant disruption to supplies of essential foodstuffs and other necessary resources.

- **Species extinction and a reduction in bio-diversity:** at the very least, future generations will have to contend with a world that is monochrome by comparison with today, reflected in a much reduced variety of plants and animals.

- **Population pressure and the resulting rise in disease, and food and water shortages:** at the very least, future generations will have to contend with continuing and worsening images of poverty and periodic pandemic health scares.

- **The impact of War and Terrorism:** at the very least, future generations will have to contend with a less secure world in which random acts of violence and images of untold misery become commonplace.

If you're in any doubt about the seriousness of any of these challenges, Appendix 1 provides a more detailed summary of each.

Guessing the Future:

The phrases are all too familiar. They are like old friends in whose company we feel comfortable and who we know will never demand too much of us. Yet any of these challenges, if fully realised, would spell the end of Western civilisation as we know it and could threaten the long-term viability of our species. Worse still is the truly frightening recognition that these threats do not exist in isolation, but intermesh in a way that suggests they are likely to prompt and reinforce one another – climate change will increase the rate and ferocity of floods and storms which will, in turn, exacerbate food shortages, leading to further incursions into the remaining wildernesses, driving animal and plant species to the wall; population movements due to flooding and natural disasters and the need to keep oil and gas supplies flowing will increase the likelihood of war, etc., etc. (the advent of "peak oil" – the point at which production peaks and begins to decline, no matter what the demand (see pages 114 and 167) – will cause great economic and social pain, especially in the West.

We should be wary about trying to predict the future. Just as the pioneers of the Industrial Revolution could hardly have imagined our world, so we can be sure that life in a hundred years' time will bear little relation to the assumptions we make today. That is the nature of the human condition. Each generation takes the world as it finds it and stamps its own imprint on the reality that it takes for granted. We may be exaggerating the problems that face us, or we may not. That is something that we will never know. However, the seriousness of the predictions that are being made for each of these challenges suggests that, at the very least, we should be acting as if they, or something like them, might happen.

What then must we do? The way we live and act is currently the major factor in each of these challenges. Climate change is directly linked to the emission of greenhouse gases produced by our addiction to fossil fuels; our need to house and feed an increasing population in ever more luxury is putting intolerable strains on our ecosystems; our unwillingness to control our own fertility means the world's population will continue to grow for the foreseeable future creating political instability and demands for further economic growth; the rate at which we are using up the Earth's resources and the manner in which we extract and dispose of them has a direct and devastating impact on the environment; the struggle to maintain and improve national living standards vis-à-vis other countries, combine with the tensions produced by the other challenges to create distrust, enmity and fear, the factors that lead inevitably to war.

In short, the way we live today is unsustainable. It would be unsustainable even without the challenges that our reckless pursuit of material advancement has created. It has been esti-mated, for example, that if we aspired to a world in which every person enjoyed the standard of living of the average American, we would need six back-up planets[1] – there simply aren't the resources to go round. So, we either continue with a system that creates haves and have-nots (85% of the world's economic wealth is owned by just 20% of its population – the poorest 20%, by comparison, own 2%[2]) and try to live with the consequences, or we learn to live in a different way.

Part of the solution, therefore, is to begin to live sustainably. But what does that mean in practice? Since the 1987 Brundtland Commission report defined sustainability as "development that meets the needs of the present without compromising the ability of future generations to meet their own needs"[3], a whole industry in definitions has been created, but four themes are common to most:-

- **The maintenance of a quality of life both now and into the future:** a sustainable future is not some joyless vision of munching root vegetables and freezing in an unheated hovel. *Sustainability is about re-examining what a quality of life means* and that certainly implies a different set of priorities to those we subscribe to today. Different sorts of things will be produced in different ways, for example, but a return to the Dark Ages it is not. In fact, it can be argued that a collapse of society is more likely if we bury our heads in the sand, do nothing and just continue in the way we are at present. And that will certainly restrict the ability of future generations to meet *their* needs.

- **Maintaining that quality of life in a just and equitable manner across the globe:** war and terrorism are bad news for sustainability not just in terms of the people caught up in the death and destruction being wreaked upon them but because the military machine is interested solely in the bangs per buck its technology can produce. Sustainability features way down, if at all, on its list of priorities. War is also, by definition, a waste of the Earth's precious resources. *Sustainability is about re-examining our relationships with our neighbours*, some of whom happen to live on the other side of the planet.

- **Maintaining that quality of life within the capacities of local, regional and global ecosystems to support it:** we must all recognise both the importance of our ecosystems and the limits that must not be passed if they are to be nurtured and sustained. More importantly we must learn to live that understanding in our day-to-day existence. Until very recently, the ecosystem wasn't even part of the equation; if an entrepreneur wanted to build a factory they found the cheapest, most cost-effective solution and then got on with it, never mind the fact that the river into which the factory's waste products were dumped died as a consequence. In future, the fact that different parts of the world – and different places within each region – can sustain certain activities and not others will have to be part of our decision-making. *Sustainability is about re-examining our relationship with the world around us.*

• **Taking the long-term view:** for a process to be sustainable in the here and now is not necessarily the same thing as it being sustainable for ever. Energy sources that are renewable, for example, are so called because they originate, in the main, from the sun. We don't have to do anything, the energy is just there and will continue as long as it continues to shine. In the terms of our current economic thinking, therefore, the energy is free. It's when we start trying to collect or harvest it that we begin to incur cost. Technology is required and that means we have to expend energy to build and maintain the machines that are going to convert that free source into a form that is useful – electricity for example. Some processes might require more energy to produce and service the machine than it is actually capable of collecting over its operational lifetime. That is clearly unsustainable and demonstrates that we need to look at the technologies we use in a much wider context than we do at present, including the costs (not just economic) of disposing of a machine at the end of its useful life. *Sustainability is about re-examining our relationship with technology.*

We now understand something of the challenges we face and have the beginnings of a conceptual framework (sustainability) with which to sketch in the kind of changes that need to take place if we are to meet them. Two things should be apparent by now. The challenges exist right now and are potentially disastrous to humankind in their impact. Secondly, the changes to the way we live that are required to meet them are of an order of magnitude that hasn't happened since the Industrial Revolution; we are not talking simply of new technologies or more effective controls, we are facing an entirely new way of relating to one another and to the environment we share and depend on. *In short, we are addressing the question of how to live securely and harmoniously on this crowded planet in a way that ensures future generations will be able to enjoy at least the same quality of life.*

Decisions, Decisions:

That is a huge agenda and the truth is that we are hardly scratching the surface: we've hardly begun. Which prompts the question – why isn't more being done? After all, the knowledge exists and we have more material resources at our disposal than at any time in human history. So what is stopping us?

We aren't good at change. That is the real nub of the problem. As individuals, we are creatures of habit and are most comfortable following familiar routines. To do something different, we first need an incentive to act – either a positive vision of what will result or, more simply, the lure of a reward. We then have to make a conscious decision to do it and, if that something different requires a major change in the way we think and act, then there will be all sorts of inbuilt resistances to taking even the first step: we lead busy lives, we don't have time; the issues appear too complex, we need to think about them; we don't know where to start; we don't believe it'll make that much difference, so why bother; we'll start tomorrow, etc., etc.

When that kind of change is required at a societal level, the inertia in the system is even harder to overcome. Decisions are taken at all levels in society and the larger and more complex the social structures are, the more complex and potentially confusing and contradictory the systems of decision-making become. It is not unusual, for example, for different government departments to introduce initiatives that have the effect of contradicting one another.

In this instance, however, it is not just a question of inertia. We have to face the disturbing possibility that the system we call democracy is simply incapable of rising to the challenges we face. Worse still, our faith that someone – or some group – has the ability to change things if only they can be convinced of the need may prove to be just that, a belief that has no basis in reality. We may be on course for disaster, like a *Titanic* sailing full steam ahead with the band playing, and quite unable to do anything about it.

But we are getting ahead of ourselves, perhaps even jumping to alarmist conclusions. We need to go back to first principles and understand why some things happen and others don't. The term *governance* is shorthand for the multi-faceted nature of decision-making in any society and can be defined as "the sum of the many ways individuals and institutions, both public and private, manage their common affairs"[4]. It is far more than "government" and its narrow role of law-making, or even the political process (systems of voting, impact of interest groups, financing of political parties, etc.), covering everything from the way our public and private institutions function to the forms of voluntary association available to individuals and the way we ourselves behave on a day-to-day basis. From this perspective it is possible to see that, for a government policy to work, it has to be taken on board and lived at all levels. If people don't want to do something, no amount of legislation will change that. Conversely, if people sense a need for change that isn't reflected in governmental and institutional priorities, the impact of individual action is lessened.

The reasons given for the collapse of civilisations are many and varied – unsustainable agricultural methods, disease, war, lack of leadership, etc. All of those factors and more will have played a part, but, in the final analysis, civilisations fail because their governance is unable to rise to new and unexpected challenges. If farming practices were unsustainable it was open to people to do things differently; a lack of leadership may have been due to patterns of power that weren't flexible enough to allow the right person to emerge at the right time, that too could have been changed ...

Historically, new civilisations often appear to emerge despite themselves. Usually they are blessed with some natural or technological advantage that gives them a head start, but they also need a sense of purpose that is shared by at least a significant proportion of the population. That doesn't just happen and it doesn't necessarily emerge from the ruling elites who would normally be expected to set the scene in terms of what is considered important and who determine how things should be done. There has to be a perception, perhaps only in a few minds initially, of possibilities outside those normally considered appropriate, and a degree of freedom that allows those individuals and groups to look at what is around them through new eyes and to experiment with new ways of doing things. Not all of these initiatives work but, collectively and over time, they can forge a new way of viewing the world.

Take the Industrial Revolution, for example. It didn't happen because a government decided that, on Monday, they were going to start an Industrial Revolution. It happened because individuals saw the opportunity to do something different, something they believed was important, and there was nothing to stop them doing it. They made plenty of mistakes. In fact, people mostly saw them as eccentric – mad even – but they did change the way we all see the world around us. Once established, that shared way of looking at things released energy. There was a dynamism, a freedom of spirit, coupled to a vision of what was possible, that ensured that the myriad decisions being taken every day, quite unconsciously for the most part, reinforced rather than neutralised one another. A sort of runaway growth in enthusiasm occurred that more stagnant cultures could not resist.

One reflection of that upsurge in activity is the notion of an idea that has found its time. Language becomes more focused and specific. People have a common view of what is important. Energy is channelled to produce significant – at least for that culture – results. When we look at the ancient Greeks and Romans, the Aztecs and the Incas, the city states of the Renaissance and the empires carved out by the European nation states, we cannot but wonder at their achievements. We may not altogether understand – or approve – their actions, but there can be no doubting their vigour and belief in what they were doing.

Decision-making is akin to magnetising a piece of iron. By stroking the individual electrons into alignment, what was once an inert piece of metal becomes a source of power that has an impact on everything around it. The more the electrons can be lined up, the more powerful the effect. If decision-making at all levels in a society can be inspired by a single vision then all the myriad decisions that are being taken every day at every level in a society are more likely to be in alignment and the more coherent the effect will be. Collective energy is being focused towards a single end and there seems to be no limit to what can be achieved.

Inevitably, however, what was once vibrant, fluid and flexible tends, over time, to become rigid and formulaic, settling into a limited set of predictable responses that served well enough in the past – and may indeed be enshrined in a backward-looking veneration of the source of that civilisation's perceived greatness or destiny. In a stable world such arrangements can last a remarkably long time but, sooner or later, new challenges appear on the horizon against which any culture, unless it can re-invent and thereby renew itself, can find itself helpless. The old ways of resolving problems just don't work – may even make things worse – and there is a general retreat into denial, a pretence that nothing is wrong. Entire peoples, from the great and the good to the poorest in the land, keep their heads down, knowing at one level that they are about to be overwhelmed but, like a rabbit caught in car's headlights, quite incapable of doing anything about it.

The jury is out about where we in the West stand in relation to the challenges we face. Are we on the point of taking up the gauntlet and harnessing the almost unlimited energies of our peoples in the quest to build a sustainable world in which all can share? Or are we, despite all the warnings, unable to find the key that will open the door to a new future, condemned instead to endlessly repeat the mistakes that have brought us to where we are? The stakes could not be higher, literally the fate of the planet, and it is worth trying to get a feel for how our decision-making systems are shaping up at global, national, regional and local levels.

Global

- The United Nations, supposedly the institution created to bring the family of nations into closer harmony, is a shell, riddled with corruption and inefficiency, and capable of working only when the most powerful nations in the world will it.

- A series of World Summits on climate change (Rio, Kyoto, Johannesburg) have been impressive in terms of the rhetoric delivered, but dismally disappointing on actual results. Major polluting nations including China, Australia and the USA have consistently refused to sign up to the key Kyoto accord.

- The United States' position as the only superpower offers a unique opportunity to provide leadership, if only by example. Instead, successive administrations have followed the narrow path of self-interest. Even the peoples of its closest allies distrust and dislike what the USA is doing. Elsewhere it is seen as the embodiment of Satan.

- The global economy represents the most powerful decision-making system in the world today and it is answerable to no one, least of all to any democratically elected institution. Instead it reflects the interests of the corporate world (an extension of the developed world's power base), a set of impersonal institutions whose sole interest is in making money whatever the cost in human or environmental terms. World poverty is increasing while fifty-one of the world's hundred largest economic entities are now corporations, not countries[5] (General Motors has an annual turnover greater than the GDP of Denmark).

- The International Monetary Fund (IMF) and World Bank – the international community's mechanism for dealing with development, loans and debt repayment – promotes free trade, which means in practice the opening up of Third World markets to the unpredictability of world commodity prices, leading to spiralling debt and the forced restructuring of whole nations' economies to service the interest payments (e.g. cutting embryonic health and education programmes).

- A significant proportion of the global economy results from organised crime – drug trafficking, people, arms, fraud, etc. For example, it is estimated that the trade in illegal immigrants alone – the selling of children and young women into prostitution and babies to childless couples – is worth £4 billion a year[6]. That catalogue of human misery and degradation is equivalent to the GDP of many countries in the so-called developing world.

In terms of the conditions for a sustainable world set out above, existing systems of world governance are clearly failing. The national interests of key nations determine the agenda, which explains why inequalities in wealth continue to grow and any fine words about improving conditions for all are just that, fine words. Globalisation ensures that short-term return is the priority and, in the feverish race to fill the ever-expanding maw of consumerism, the environment, whether local, regional or global, hardly features on the balance sheet. We are being pushed ever further from the kind of sustainable world that will ensure a secure and thriving planet for future generations.

National

- A tendency towards ever more centralised systems of government, based on two, interchangeable parties funded by rich individuals and corporations who expect to see a return on their investment. Although considerable time and energy is expended in trying to capture the moral high ground, policies are often indistinguishable in practice. The faces may change but it's basically business as usual, and that business is promoting the economic growth of the home economy, at the expense of others if necessary.

- Elections held every four or five years that are more akin to beauty contests than serious debates about issues. The reality is that elections are won and lost in identifiable marginal constituencies so that, for most of the electorate, any influence they think they may exert over future policy development is illusory.

- A political elite that no longer feels it needs to listen to, let alone represent, its electorate, except in the limited context of periodic electoral campaigns.

- A continual and cynical manipulation of news and events that leads to voter apathy and a general disinclination to believe anything.

- A response to the perceived threat posed by terrorism that creates an atmosphere of fear and distrust, leading to an erosion of civil liberties and a justification for increasing secrecy on the part of government. This agenda, often used as a smokescreen for other political difficulties, leads to an acceptance of conspiracy theories and a general distrust of leaders' motives. A narrow focus on danger is reflected in the switch from a political message based on hope (we have the policies that are more likely to create a better world) to one based on fear (we have the strength and will to better protect you from the unknown and unseen).

- A national economy that sucks wealth out of poorer communities and increases the likelihood of long term dependence on benefits, grants and support (interference) from a variety of public and voluntary agencies. Formerly viable neighbourhoods can be incapacitated overnight by decisions taken centrally to build motorways, extend airports or allow the construction of a supermarket locally.

- A media that indulges in periodic feeding frenzies, arbitrarily selecting its victims and then blowing up issues out of all proportion, contributing nothing to their resolution (other than pressure on institutions both public and private to come up with instant fix solutions that are likely to compound the problem) before moving on to the next story with little regard for the mayhem left in their wake.

It is an intertwined network of power and influence obsessed with presentation, with image rather than content, whose agenda is dominated by a need to be seen to deal vigorously and effectively with real or imaginary threats, whilst accepting that the priorities of the power brokers behind the scenes can never be compromised. National governments no longer have the power to effect major changes that deviate even marginally from the general thrust of global development. They attempt to conceal their impotence behind the smoke and mirrors of spin and the ritual unveiling of new initiatives that fail to paper over the cracks and never address the fundamental questions of what they are trying to achieve.

Regional

- Public institutions (health, education, welfare, justice, etc.) are "law transmitters"; that is, they interpret and implement laws handed down to them by their political masters. As such they are top-down, command and control bureaucracies geared to ensuring that "rules" (centrally determined) are applied consistently across many outlets. By their nature they lack initiative, are unresponsive to change and disregard the unique needs of real individuals.

- As the world becomes ever faster and more complex there is an increasing need for these monoliths to co-ordinate initiatives across the board, to produce so-called joined-up government. Combined with endless restructurings aimed at making service delivery more efficient and compounded by different planning cycles, technical and professional languages, etc., plus ever more regulation, the need to implement the continuous raft of new initiatives mentioned above stretches the basically inflexible nature of these institutions to breaking point, demotivating staff and impacting on the service that the public receives (with particularly devastating results for the education system).

- To cope with the increasing complexity of everyday life there is a proliferation of non-elected bodies, often answerable only to the executive or cabinet, with powers that cut across local and regional decision-making processes, and whose contact with the people whose lives they affect is marginal.

- To remain competitive in a global marketplace devoid of regulatory machinery, private institutions get bigger and bigger (or get swallowed up by more ruthless or dynamic organisations) and, under a carefully orchestrated show of concern, find little incentive to act in an ethical or environmentally friendly way.

It is a strange world, utterly divorced from the real needs of people and driven by the shifting currents of fashion (what will sell), whether they be cultural, economic or political. It is a world that creates and justifies itself, with no clear vision or sense of purpose, fired only by the need for self-protection in a hostile and complex world where the chances of being caught out appear to be ever increasing.

Local

- Local communities and neighbourhoods, in the sense of sharing some sort of identification with and responsibility for one another, have disappeared with frightening speed over the past fifty years.

- Individuals now enter communities of interest – usually single-issue groupings that may be geographically diverse and have little regard for their members as rounded people having good and bad times. Work now provides the single most important source of association with others (which explains why people not in work often feel isolated and lonely), but one that is limited by the continual shift in personnel and where one's own long-term position is far from secure.

- Local shops and amenities – where local people would once have met one another – are disappearing to be replaced by supermarkets and out-of-town shopping malls, all requiring the use of a car.

- The speed and pressure of life mean that individuals increasingly relate to one another in terms of the roles they play rather than who they are as people, resulting in a weakening of the social fabric.

- The lack of identification between people is reflected in the increasing resort to the Law as the preferred option when trying to resolve disputes, reinforced by a broadening of laws relating to what would once have been seen as private behaviour.

- Children now rarely participate meaningfully in their neighbourhoods and grow up with little understanding of community and the importance to their own self-development of engaging collaboratively with others. Their view of social reality is more likely to be conditioned by television and the internet.

In short, we are increasingly living as isolated individuals who have forgotten how to act collectively for the common good. People's lives are dominated by the big battalions who treat us as if we didn't exist, and our sphere of action has been reduced to that of consumers, foot soldiers in the relentless battle to sell more, quicker.

Where Do We Go from Here?

From this brief overview of the increasingly complex decision making systems that make our society what it is, we can begin to understand why we seem to rushing headlong down a road that is not sustainable, why there is a deafening silence about the enormity of the challenges we face, and why there appears to be no obvious alternative. At every level the opportunities for real people to say "hang on, this is not the way it should be" are being reduced; real people have become irrelevant to a leviathan careering remorselessly along according to its own priorities and logic.

It is difficult, if not impossible, for any change that is not led by fashion or a manipulated public opinion (themselves the product of hugely expensive, interlocking processes driven by the need to sell everything from cars to votes) to get a toehold. We're all swept along on a tsunami-like wave: we get busier and busier and achieve less and less. We're running just to stand still. And it is hard to see any other way, or even where that other way might come from; the system, although out of control, is self-serving and self-perpetuating.

That is because we no longer share a vision about what is important. Our social magnet has no charge and, as a consequence, we lack that simple, focused language that might propel united action. We live in confused and confusing times; all the hallmarks, in short, of a civilisation incapable of rising to the challenges it faces.

So where must we look for answers? First, we must acknowledge that there is a real and pressing problem, and then feel sufficiently angry or fearful about it that we want things to change. Second, that anger/fear has to be channelled into understanding more about the nature of the problem and how we have come to be in the position we are. Third, we need to explore how our ideas change and how that is then translated into action. Fourth, we need to have an alternative way of looking at the world, offering a positive vision of the kind of sustainable world that can be enjoyed by our descendants in perpetuity and that will provide the energy to overcome our inbuilt resistance to change. And then we must act!

That is the agenda of this book. The way forward will not be easy but we have the opportunity, given to few generations, to truly change the world.

If you're already convinced that fundamental change is required, go straight to Chapter 5; if not, keep reading!

2

It's the Economy Stupid![1]

Good decision-making is a balancing act, making choices in one area while keeping one's eye on the bigger picture to ensure that the consequences of one's actions do not impact unfavourably elsewhere. As individuals we depend on feedback loops, opportunities to test our decisions in practice and fine-tune them to meet the exigencies of the real world; the more attuned to them we are, the more likely it is that we will make good decisions. In most instances we can literally see the impact we are having on others and, hopefully, we are sensitive and flexible enough to modify our behaviour accordingly.

Conversely, one sign of bad decision-making is when we pursue an objective and don't have the information systems that allow us to see the problems that result from our choices. It's as if we're blind to what is going on around us. We plough on regardless and ignore the fact that the harm we are causing is happening and that it keeps on happening – until a crisis occurs, and we have no option but to sit up and take notice; by which time, of course, it may be too late. A closed, self-contained system has been created, referring only to itself and apparently impervious to what is going on outside. The bigger such systems are, the easier it is for them to insulate themselves from the real world and the more damage they can do.

Observing our society in action, it is hard to escape the conclusion that this ostrich like behaviour is exactly what is happening everywhere, for much of the time. In terms of scale some of these systems are huge, spanning the globe, but, once you know what to look for, you will see this deadly dynamic everywhere, as a brief look at the key areas of economic, political and social activity will demonstrate.

The economy is the sum total of a myriad of decisions that are being taken every second of every day. Some of those decisions are naturally more weighty than others and will have potentially far greater impact. The decision of a President of the USA to purchase a new weapons system or a Chief Executive of a multinational corporation to relocate activities in a country on the other side of the world will affect more people than an individual's decision to buy a new washing machine. But the cumulative impact of individual consumers is not insignificant and has been known to unseat powerful executives; equally, our perceptions of how the economy is performing for us continue to give politicians sleepless nights. That dance between the powerful individual and the power of the undifferentiated mass, and how the two can become locked in a destructive spiral, is typified in the supermarket.

Supermarkets are a consumer's dream come true. To be able to satisfy all one's needs under one roof, cheaply, quickly and without the hassle of having to maintain an ongoing relationship with a shopkeeper, fits our high-speed world like a glove. It's just so convenient and natural. We're in control. Or so we think.

The marketplace is all about providing consumers with what they want. In that sense it is morally neutral: if people suddenly want gas-guzzlers and patio heaters then such items will miraculously appear. We are increasingly cash-rich and time-poor, but we also want to make our money go as far as possible, so we can keep up with the latest must-have gadgetry. As a consequence, convenience and cheapness in all aspects of life are at a premium. Organisations that make it quick and easy for us to do what we want at a price we regard as affordable will win every time and supermarkets aim to do just that.

Considerable time, effort and planning goes into ensuring that the shelves are always stocked with the maximum choice and laid out in ways that tempt us to buy. Price cuts are the name of the game while the range of goods and services goes on expanding. Advertising subtly hints at the lifestyles we aspire to – succulent food served by famous chefs, or streetwise shoppers who know a bargain when they see one – and everything combines to suggest that what we experience is almost a public service and laid on for our personal benefit.

The reality, of course, is that we are being gently corralled into accepting the agenda of the supermarkets. We buy the goods that it is profitable for them to sell and, while the range on offer may get bigger, the choice within individual items is restricted to fewer and fewer big-name brands. If you want anything that isn't routinely stocked (environmentally friendly household products, an organic breakfast cereal produced by a local manufacturer) you have to go elsewhere. In that sense our individual wishes are simply being ignored. And if we complain about the service we do receive (an item temporarily out of stock, food we discover to be off when we get it home) we are likely to receive the standard, well-crafted apology and some token compensation – and we accept because we have little real choice in the matter. A national, if not multinational, player against a single individual is no contest and, besides, life's too short to fight every battle; it's best to just shrug and get on with it.

On the face of it, the trade-off is simple; we get cheapness and convenience and, in return, the supermarkets control everything else. But life is never simple. Behind the cheerful shop front lies a complex and far-flung system of decision-making that has only two aims: to grab more market share and increase profitability. And that is the Achilles heel of the whole setup because the supermarket boards are running scared; scared that we might take our custom to a rival or, worse still, that a rival might steal a march on them with some new marketing ploy (supermarkets become hypermarkets become shopping malls, etc.).

That fear drives them to continually look for ways to reduce their overheads which implies a combination of sourcing the cheapest products from anywhere in the world and expanding their operation to benefit from economies of scale. The market-place has become so cut-throat that there is no alternative and, if that creates a whole series of negative consequences, then so be it; there is an expensive public relations industry to head off potential criticism. Both we and the supermarket chains collude in a fantasy of guilt-free and problem-free shopping.

It is worth reflecting what our love affair with supermarkets is costing (Britain's shoppers spent around £70 billion on food in 2005, 56% of which was in supermarkets[2]):-

- **Green House Gas Emissions and Climate change:** sourcing cheap food and goods from all over the world means extended supply chains; it has been estimated that every item on a supermarket shelf in the UK has travelled an average of 1000 miles[3]; supermarkets are sited away from residential areas which means that people have to use a car to access them.

- **Agricultural crisis:** the demand for cheap food has margin-alised small farmers (numbers in the UK declined from 82,000 in 2001 to 68,000 in 2004[4]) and encouraged the spread of huge agribusiness concerns dependent on mono-culture, artificial fertilisers and high-tech equipment, all of which contribute directly to a loss in the land's long-term fer-tility. As a direct consequence of the globalisation of indus-trial agriculture we use ten calories of petrochemicals to produce one calorie of food on our tables.

- **Reduction in choice and loss of diversity:** four varieties of apple and three of potato comprise 90% of the UK market today compared with fifty well-known varieties of apple and thirty of potato in the 1950s[5]); orchards, once the pride of England, have been grubbed up and we import most of our apples. Intensive farming methods used in meat and dairy production lead to unhealthy and stressed animals, which is reflected in the quality of the product that reaches the public (there used to be around twenty different types of dual purpose (beef/milk), regionally distinct breeds of cattle in the UK – they have been replaced with just one, the Friesian

Holstein – "lousy milk, lousy meat ... but lots of it"[6]); put simply, we have lost the ability to discriminate, we accept what we're given.

- **Animal welfare:** to increase yields means keeping cows indoors and feeding them mown grass, rearing ducks that never swim on water (they would normally spend up to 80% of their lives afloat[7]), etc., etc.

- **Waste:** it is estimated that as much as a third of all food produced for supermarkets is thrown away, not because it isn't fit to eat but because the appearance of the product doesn't comply with the strict guidelines laid down by the buyers. Cauliflowers, for example, must have near-flawless leaves even though these are not eaten[8].

- **Reduction in competition:** the growth in the number and size of supermarkets has spelt the death knell for local shops, especially greengrocers, butchers and bakers, where a range of, often, local products were available; loss of local shops means people getting in their car every time they need to purchase food, however small the quantities. It also further fractures local communities that are being dispersed by the ever-quickening pace of life and increasing mobility.

- **Unsafe food:** there has been one food scare after another associated with the systems of food production necessary to keep prices low. Worse still, all the major supermarkets use the same networks of producers, distributors and manufacturers, so a problem anywhere along the line (contamination of an ingredient that ends up in many different products, for example) is likely to affect them all.

- **Distortion of the political process:** as large organisations with access to the best legal brains, supermarkets can circumvent or wear down the planning processes so that new complexes are built against the wishes of local people.

The list is long and getting longer. In short, supermarkets are bad for the environment, our food, our animals and our farmers. More than that, it is clear that a way of doing things that has become central to the way we live, that makes complete sense economically, is perfectly legal, and gives people what they say they want is contributing directly to the challenges we face. It is a closed, self-contained system.

And, in common with all such systems, it appears to be unstoppable. More and more supermarkets are planned or being built. An immense amount of time, talent and resources is being poured into an activity that is unsustainable. The issue becomes how we free up that energy and put it to more constructive use. The supermarkets themselves aren't going to change what they're doing – operating within a closed system makes that very hard anyway; governments, for the reasons explored in the next chapter, are equally impotent; which leaves us, the consumers – real people who can literally change the world if enough of us decide to act.

There are many other examples of this kind of closed-system madness, the pursuit of goals that lead directly to mounting pressure on the environment or human health and well-being – systems that trap people in poverty, create the conditions where obesity can be a sensible life choice, promote air travel in a way that will inevitably bring the problems associated with our car culture, and put a premium on hi-tech, spiralling military expenditure, to mention but a few.

Closed systems take on a life of their own and it is often difficult to see how to escape the power of their distorted logic. The need to find a way of unravelling their smothering tentacles is greater than ever, and to do that we need to take a calm, clear look at the world we take so much for granted.

The Obvious Question is "Why?"

Given that the basic function of the economy is to meet human needs (and, in a democracy, that theoretically means everybody's needs, not just those of the rich and powerful), how is it that it seems to be failing so spectacularly?

Well, the simple answer is that the world economy is the biggest closed system of them all.

One of the features of a closed system is that it appears to be a totally natural state of affairs, like gravity, and we take it for granted.

It is in precisely these circumstances that we need what might be called a Divine Right of Kings Moment, one of those pivot points in history that change the way people view the world around them. The English Civil War (1642-1649) was fought not about the right of Charles I (1600-1649) to rule but about his relationship with his people and, specifically, the parliament that represented them. The problem was that, although beaten, Charles refused to accept that his role could be anything other than ordained by, and answerable directly to, God. Just what do you do with a recalcitrant king when there is a prevailing and self-evident belief in the God-given right of kingship; when you yourself cannot comprehend a future without a king, so natural a state of affairs does it appear?

From his defeat at the Battle of Naseby in June 1645 until his execution on 30 January 1649, Parliament wrestled with that problem, and it was only when Charles precipitated a second civil war that the decision to remove him once and for all was seriously confronted. Even then, only fifty-nine members of the court signed the death warrant and there was a general expectation in the land that God would avenge the blasphemy of killing his anointed. Whether that happened or not depends on your point of view. What is not disputable, however, is that English society was changed for ever; any rights that kings might enjoy would be determined by earthly considerations rather than divine.

We need to look at the global economy in the same light and accept that it is a human construct. If it works, fine, but if it doesn't we have to find ways of getting rid of it, end of story.

We live in a society dominated by debt (the total value of credit card debt in Britain is currently £55bn[9]). As with so many aspects of the way we live today, that statement seems so self-evident that it requires an effort of imagination to realise that there are alternatives. Over the many millennia that humans existed as hunter-gatherers, for example, concepts such as debt, repayments, interest and repossession would have been meaningless. It's easy to romanticise the past but, in this context, it's worth reflecting that quality of life was limited not by what could be afforded but by a group's skill and imagination in terms of building shelters, making tools, finding food, dancing and telling stories. Basic needs took only three to four hours a day to meet and the rest of the time was devoted to their relationships and enjoying themselves. On rare occasions they might need to barter with neighbours, but for most of the time they were indebted only in the sense of mutual obligation. They lived in harmony with their surroundings or, at the very least, their activities had no long-term consequences for the environment they shared with the rest of creation.

By contrast, we need something called "money" for almost everything we use and consume, from water to food, from housing to just getting around, from keeping in touch with others to the way we entertain ourselves. It has reached the stage where most of our time is devoted to getting the money required to meet our needs, and our relationships with one another have suffered as a consequence: we simply don't have a relationship with our environment and are in danger of destroying it as a result.

A closer look at the way the economy works may give us some clues as to how this state of affairs has come about.

The need for money and how we obtain it determines the way our lives are shaped. For most of us, we have to do something called "work", giving up our time to undertake some activity, usually in some place other than our home and neighbourhood, in return for which we receive "money". The problem is that the money we receive isn't usually enough for us to meet our needs in a way that satisfies us. We might want to buy a bigger house, own a new car, take an expensive holiday, or start up in business on our own.

So we have to get hold of some additional money, which is called "borrowing". We could ask a friend to help us out, but the more usual course is to approach a "bank" which is a place that specialises in handling money. Banks aren't philanthropic enterprises, they're "businesses" owned by their "shareholders" who want a "return" on their "investment". They also have people like us, "employees", who have to be paid for the work they do in helping us with our money. In other words, in giving us something we want, banks expect us to "pay" for the "services" they provide, and we're all so familiar with paying "interest" on the money we borrow that we don't give it a second thought (it is worth noting that all the words in quotation marks are human constructs, i.e. they relate to the way we choose to behave as human beings rather than to any objective or immutable natural law).

At this point is necessary to make a distinction between "interest" and "usury"[10]. If I ask to borrow some money from you then, assuming you have it, you might choose to lend it to me – or you might not. You might have been about to redecorate your house, so lending it to me might mean you having to put your plans on hold. In which case, it would seem reasonable that I should compensate you in some way; I might, for example, help with the painting while I'm paying you back the money, or I might buy you a present in gratitude. These are forms of interest, a recognition that you have been put out in some way in helping me.

When the bank lends me money, however, it is not inconvenienced in any way – not even by the decision about whether to lend to me or someone else – because it effectively creates the loan out of thin air (95% of all money that is loaned out is issued in this way – it is new money[11]). Thus any charges I have to pay the bank (apart from a tiny element that reflects the cost of setting up and administering the loan) are not to compensate them for any difficulties my borrowing may cause them, but reflect the bank's ability to make money simply by creating it. In fact it disadvantages the bank when I don't borrow because then they can't create any extra money, so they can't charge for it (total profits for the top five UK high street banks in 2005 was £33bn[12]). In other words, the bank is profiting from its position. That is usury and the importance of this distinction will become clear shortly. For now, it is worth noting that the three "religions of the book" – Judaism, Christianity and Islam – have all prohibited usury. Dante placed usurers on a lower circle in hell than murderers.

How do banks create money out of thin air? First, we need to understand that this magical process has nothing to do with conventional money in the sense of dollars, pounds and euros that we can hold in our hands. We have entered a non-cash economy in which virtual money is flashing round the world in millionths of a second, twenty-four seven. It has no substance and doesn't even necessarily relate to the exchange of real goods and services.

Once upon a time banks would literally use the money they had available to make a loan (money that had been deposited with them by people who had more than they needed at present) so, providing the bank got its assessment of risk right (which, in practice, meant that only the rich could borrow), it could always be confident that it wouldn't run out of money. Increasing demand led to increasing sophistication and, as an additional safeguard, a proportion of a bank's reserves in the form of gold would be held in a central bank run by the government who also controlled the money supply by determining the rate at which bank notes and cash could be issued into circulation. It was as safe as the Bank of England.

Those days have long since gone and banks now create the money they lend with little or nothing to back it up. They don't even create real cash, merely manipulate systems of electronic accounts. Banks have an international reach and are competing with one another for business, so borrowing has become easier and easier (banks creating more and more money to bring in more profit and expand their business).

When the economy is growing there are few problems: the amount of new money being created always exceeds the amount of debt being paid off (there will inevitably be failures, but any money owing can be recouped elsewhere or written off as bad debt). Interest rates are usually low and the only fear is the economy overheating (i.e. growing unsustainably and leading to run-away inflation). Profits and confidence are both high.

In bad times, however, the reverse happens. Banks become more cautious, so there is less new money being created than the total debt that is due. There is a limit to the cut-backs existing debtors can make (creating the space in their finances to enable them to continue paying off their debt and the interest that continues to accrue) and, as a consequence, people and businesses become increasingly desperate in their attempts to grab what they can from the now limited amount of money in circulation. Inevitably, many fail to make enough to cover their repayments, and their assets – houses, businesses, etc. – are repossessed. Because general confidence is on the wane, however, there are fewer people looking to buy things and less money with which to do it, so the value of those assets is less than it used to be, and the banks have to accept what they can get, which usually means they don't get back what they originally lent. Banks become even more reluctant to lend and there is now a real danger of a downward spiral turning into a nosedive as more and more businesses collapse and reduce the chances of the remainder being able to turn the situation round. It is the classic scenario for a slump.

Avoiding a crash is the Holy Grail of economists and finance ministers around the world. The global economy is certainly more robust than at the time of the Depression in the 1930s, but it is based on the need for continual growth – to service the loans that the banks have already encouraged us to take out by creating yet more non-cash money and further boosting their profits. It is a system that has to go on running just to keep up with itself. And it is ultimately unsustainable if only because the earth's resources are finite (as disposable incomes increase in real terms, both in the affluent and developing worlds, so does the demand for goods and services and there is no natural limit to the process).

To keep the economy growing – ensuring that there is more money being created than the repayments on the debt incurred to produce that growth, while at the same time avoiding inflationary pressures – we have created a world in which we must accumulate ever more stuff (most of it on credit). The fact that 99% of the materials used in the production and sale of a product in the USA are thrown away within six weeks of sale[13] is an irrelevance. We are consumers and, like addicts, have to keep feeding the habit. Usury (the profiting from money) is not only bleeding us dry, it is destroying the planet.

Just in case you think all this competition benefits the consumer in terms of ever-lower prices, think again. When you buy anything at all you are paying the aggregated interest that has accumulated along the production chain. Producers of raw materials (farmers or miners) pay interest on the machinery they employ; they have to pass that on to someone. In the first instance, that someone is the shipper who moves the raw materials to where they can be processed – they also have trucks, ships and aeroplanes they must borrow money to keep moving. And so it goes on, from producer to assembler, from assembler to wholesaler, from wholesaler to retailer; and, finally, on to you. At each stage there are further transport costs to be factored into the equation and more loans to be financed. Not surprisingly, the major element in the cost of some items is the interest that has been paid all the way down the line.

The framework within which this miracle of endless growth is achieved is called the free market and is based on the premise that everyone should be free to sell anything to anyone. If I have an idea about something that other people might want, then providing I have the wherewithal (the materials, machinery and skill, or else the money to buy them through other people investing in my scheme), no obstacles should be put in the way of my producing it. If I succeed then I am considered a winner, if I fail, well at least I tried. It's as simple as that.

Reality, of course, is never that simple. For a start I'm usually in competition with other producers, which means that we're all continually trying to get our money to work harder for us to gain a competitive edge. That implies reducing fixed costs (particularly labour – hence the pressure to outsource anything and everything to cheaper labour markets), introducing more efficient technology or different materials, operating on a larger scale and generally doing anything that will improve productivity (the cost of each unit of production). Naturally, this requires yet more investment (loans), as does the opening up of new markets and products (fuelled by the ever restless goddess of fashion) to satisfy the growth imperative.

Not surprisingly, we have reached a point where only a global marketplace can contain the forces produced by this increasingly frenetic need to buy and sell. If that means farmers in the developing world being forced off self-sufficient farms to create the space for cash crops, or the rain forest being destroyed, then so be it. That's the way the world is and, besides, the alternative (global economic meltdown) is unthinkable. If that isn't an example of a closed system that is incapable of facing up to the damage it is creating then I don't know what is.

If that doesn't make you angry, it should.

The World is Their Oyster

In fact, the situation is even worse. As we have seen, most of the wealth that is being created is virtual rather than real. Twenty-four seven, almost unimaginable sums move around the world and they have long since ceased to represent actual goods and services, reflecting rather speculation upon speculation. It has been estimated that 98% of all foreign exchange transactions, for example, are purely speculative in nature; essentially betting on which way national currencies are going to move[14]. When you add in futures trading, derivatives and hedge funds – not to mention the money laundering associated with organised crime – it is hard to avoid the impression that the global economy is more like a casino than a mechanism for helping real people enrich their lives. As such, it is essentially unstable and depends, once again, on continuing growth in the world's markets. All the engines of commerce are moving us in that direction and the juggernaut is now so big and moving so fast that it is quite incapable of taking into account the damage that is being caused in the process.

One of the justifications of the free market is that it is an impersonal instrument of economic health. For that very reason the medicine has to be applied ruthlessly. There will be casualties, but they are both inevitable and necessary for the fitness of the whole, so we shouldn't spend too much time worrying about them. It has no favourites and thus perfectly embodies the American Dream of being able to rise from rags to riches (getting to be President may be a bit more difficult – see next chapter) with the comforting implication that virtue triumphs in the end. It is a neo-Darwinian vision in which the struggle for survival takes on global dimensions. The fact that the USA is clearly winning merely demonstrates and reinforces America's view that it is the world's natural leader.

If things worked like that in practice, it is a point of view; not one that those who believe in liberty and democracy might find it easy to subscribe to, but a valid point of view none the less. Reality, however, is far removed from the theory, and the system serves the rich and powerful, working for only a small proportion of the world's population and effectively excluding the rest. It has already been suggested that there is nothing new in that and, if it wasn't for the fact that the system is destroying the world, maybe one's energies would be better channelled into getting one's share of the spoils.

But it is destroying the world and the lie needs to be exposed. As an example of how the system favours the rich one only has to look at how credit is extended to poorer nations, theoretically to allow them to develop and compete effectively in world markets. For a start, credit is only available in certain areas, particularly in agriculture and light industry, and on certain terms, and guess where the interest repayments go – you've got it, straight to the banks run by and for the rich countries. And what does that credit buy? Machinery, pesticides, seed and know-how, which are produced predominantly by companies owned by multinational corporations with their headquarters and investors in New York, London, Paris and Berlin. It is hardly surprising, therefore, to discover that five such companies control seventy-five per cent of the international grain trade, six account for 75% of the world's pesticide market and Monsanto alone is responsible for 91% of global genetically modified (GM) seed. When you look at specific crops, two companies dominate the sale of half the world's bananas and three account for 85% of the world's tea; Wal-Mart controls 40% of Mexico's entire retail food sector[15]. These companies have been able to expand dramatically over the past decade aided by the so-called liberalisation of international trade.

Not only do poorer nations have to service their debt to these rich world organisations, they have to do it at the most exposed end of the international market: they are in competition with other primary producers across the world and, when the world economy shows signs of turning down, it is always agriculture that gets hit first, with prices tumbling and what was previously profitable no longer worth producing. To add insult to injury, the rich world thinks nothing of dumping its surpluses of tariff protected foodstuffs on the poor, thereby wrecking fragile local markets and creating a dispossessed urban underclass (farm subsidies in the OECD – the Organisation for Economic Co-operation and Development, basically the most powerful developed nations – for the year 2003 were equivalent to a massive 48% of all agricultural production; down just three percentage points – from 51% – in 1986-8, despite all the development rounds and trade negotiations in between[16]).

And when poor nations default on their repayments, organisations like the IMF feel perfectly justified in moving in to "restructure" the debt, requiring the kind of butchery of basic education and health care services that would cause riots if attempted in a Western nation. Poor economies will stay at the bottom of the pile – which is exactly where they need to be if we are to continue accumulating our stuff at their expense.

It is hardly surprising that democracy can't flourish in such conditions because they represent economic imperialism at its most naked. All previous systems of gathering stuff (over and above the basics needed to sustain life) have depended on one group's ability to exploit others – through direct force or its threat, taxes, war, technology or slavery. In that sense our civilisation is no different. We are all aristocrats now in the West, squeezing our wealth from an impoverished peasantry. Unlike our forebears in the Middle Ages, however, our peasants are conveniently out of sight on the other side of the world and we don't have to confront the consequences of our behaviour on a daily basis. The lifestyles we enjoy are predicated on the grinding poverty that is the feature of so much of our world. It is obscene and we are all implicated.

This overview of the world economy is inevitably simplistic but, in moving from the individual to the global level, it hopefully demonstrates how interconnected the whole system is. The interest we pay on our individual loan can be and is used to finance credit that funds a range of dysfunctional activities – from GM seed to armaments, from supermarkets to sweatshops – merely because they make economic good sense (i.e. they produce a profit).

The reality is that we have all been reduced to minuscule pieces of information in the global marketplace. We no longer have meaning. Money has become both abstract and virtual, and is no longer engaged with the world of real people. It has become detached and its way of working has gained a spurious objectivity that allows people to make decisions that are injurious to health and happiness and, ultimately, to the wellbeing of the planet itself.

Above all it has become so large and all encompassing that there seems to be no other way of doing things. How could we survive without our credit cards and all the things that they can buy?

To have faith in such a system is like continuing to believe that kingship is divinely ordained in the face of the evident death, poverty and misery it is causing. It doesn't have to be like that. The only true impediment to seeing an alternative to what appears natural and god-given lies within ourselves and our inability to think outside the box. Sometimes we just have to think the unthinkable. That is when we are close to a Divine Right of Kings Moment.

3

Democracy – Ideal or Bum Deal?

If shining the light of freedom into the darkest places on Earth is to be anything other than one more in a long line of pretexts for imposing the West's viewpoint on the rest of the world – ultimately for its own benefit – then we need to be very confident that the democratic ideals we are exporting will indeed deliver the goods. Not just in terms of improving quality of life and human happiness, but also in terms of a people's ability to rise to the challenges of sustainability, we have to believe that our institutions are delivering, or are capable of delivering, those benefits to us, here and now. The fact that we are only scratching the surface of the sustainability agenda should not be taken as an indication that our basic framework is irredeemably flawed, but it does suggest that we ought to be looking at the beam in our own eye before attempting to remove the mote in our neighbours'.

What Western civilisation says it believes and what it then does in practice are often poles apart and usually justified by that old chestnut, the nature of realpolitik; the limitations imposed by the realities of having to operate in a far from perfect world. That is one way of looking at the legacy of destruction, looting and exploitation that continues to be one of the main features of our impact on the wider world. Another is to recognise that there are two opposing legacies lodged deep in the Western psyche – those that have come down to us from the classical ages of Greece and Rome; democracy versus empire.

One only has to visit the ruins of the glory that was Rome to see the blueprint for much that is so familiar to us today that we hardly give it a second glance. Look around the Vatican, the capitals of Europe and the USA and you will see triumphal public buildings, monuments to dead Caesars and imperial symbolism in every direction. Even in the United States – whose republican experiment is perhaps the purest attempt to achieve the democratic ideal that we have – the Senate building in Washington DC could have been transported brick by brick from Rome, even down to the imperial eagles and fasces (the bundle of rods with an axe in the middle that denoted authority and unity).

Democracy, by contrast, has had a slow and painful evolution and, compared to the dashing image of imperial glory, is a poor and ill-formed creature struggling along in the wake of its more robust sibling. In part that is because the Western European experience following the collapse of the Roman Empire was that warfare was the only effective way to resolve disputes between peoples, requiring a strong, centralised, semi-tribal structure capable of meeting force with force. As Europe emerged from the Dark Ages, that need for clear loci of power solidified around leaders who could hold the allegiance of ever-larger groupings.

In proclaiming himself Holy Roman Emperor, Charlemagne (742-814), King of the Franks, was deliberately placing himself as heir to the classical, imperial tradition; one that was to become the norm in Europe, with kings at the apex of a clearly stratified social structure based on status, which was in turn derived from the accumulation of property and the acceptance of war as a legitimate means of getting it. At that stage, however, there was no real concept of nationhood or even of a national territory (Charlemagne divided his empire between his three sons –

although one remained the emperor, notionally overlord of the others). That came gradually and at different times in different places, and reflected a growing sense of identity based on language, as universal Latin was replaced by literatures using more local linguistic traditions (Germanic, Frankish, Italian, Celtic, Anglo-Saxon, Viking). It also depended on the gradual unification and rationalisation of tax and legal systems. Thus, England could be considered a nation as early as the tenth century (while Italy and Germany achieved political union only in the nineteenth century, despite having a rich literary heritage).

The struggle for ascendancy between these now territorial units down the centuries is what popular history is about rather than the landmarks of democratic reform (how many educated people in England have heard of the 1832 Reform Act let alone know what it introduced? – yet most will be familiar with the long litany of battles from Crécy to Agincourt, the Spanish Armada, the Civil War, Trafalgar and Waterloo. Our culture is saturated in the cult of the hero, from sport to film and television, and the young want only to be famous. Heroes have to do with empire not democracy, and our current priorities are reflected in the fact that we are now more familiar with the heroes of ancient Greece (from Odysseus to Alexander the Great – whose feats so many others have sought to emulate down the ages) than with the workings of their demos-kratos (rule by the people). If anything Greek democracy is seen as a hopelessly flawed experiment, short-lived, dependent on slaves, excluding anyone other than adult males and somehow even contriving the legalistic murder of Socrates.

And yet, throughout the history of Western civilisation (which, of course, came to include much more than just Europe) there has been a continual yearning for 'freedom', usually expressed in terms of a demand for rights. From the Peasants' Revolt to the Levellers during the English Civil War, from the American and French Revolutions to the Paris Commune and the Russian Revolution, a dream of freedom and social justice has repeatedly asserted itself. Starting in the eighteenth century and continuing to the present day, writer after writer has not only criticised – often in the starkest terms – the political and economic arrangements of the day, but expressed great optimism for the future, as if believing a brighter future that would usher in liberty and equality lay just around the corner. With the benefit of hindsight it is easy to laugh at such naivety, but are we any different? Democracy versus Empire, hope apparently springs eternal.

How Democracy Works – or Doesn't Work

For our present purposes, we need to ask how well existing forms of democracy work as decision-making processes. That will give us a clue as to how well they may be able to adapt to tackling issues of sustainability. The basic premise of democracy (rule by the people) is that good government (of the people, by the people, for the people) follows when people have a say in the decisions that affect them. How much say they should have, how often and in what size of constituency has never been specified, but underpinning the process has been the core notion of equality; each person's vote is as valuable as everyone else's. Thus, in *Rights of Man* (1791), Thomas Paine could ridicule the English Parliamentary system: "The county of Yorkshire, which contains near a million souls, sends two county members; and so does the county of Rutland which contains not a hundredth part of that number. The town of Old Sarum, which contains not three houses, sends two members; and the town of Manchester, which contains upwards of sixty thousand souls, is not admitted to send any. Is there any principle in these things?"[1]

Manchester, of course, was at forefront of the often violent campaigning that led to the great Reform Act of 1832 and paved the way to eventual universal suffrage, but the principle central to all democratic reform in the eighteenth, nineteenth and twentieth centuries was that of one person, one vote, rather than the quality and efficacy of that vote. And so it has remained. The main purpose of the Boundary Commission in the UK, for example, is to ensure that population movements do not unduly distort the number of people represented by each Member of Parliament, even though the number of voters per MP has increased considerably since the number of Members was set at 658 in 1800 at the Act of Union (it was actually *down* to 646 at the 2005 election as a result of boundary changes).

An unforeseen consequence of this obsession with "one person, one vote" has been to speed the erosion of any identification we, as individuals, might have with our communities. In England the Parish Council had been the basic unit of local government for centuries and reflected local loyalties and realities. They were swept away to be replaced by wards and constituencies (based on "fair representation") which bore little relation to existing communities: continual redrawing of boundaries has further exacerbated this trend and has helped homogenise and deaden our public life.

When the agricultural working man in Britain received the vote in 1884, the population was approximately 35 million, of whom some 4 million were then entitled to vote. The population today is around 60 million with an adult suffrage of 44 million: in other words each vote has *eleven* times less impact. An even greater growth in population has occurred in the United States (from 50 million in 1880 to 260 million today) with a proportionate diminution in the impact of each vote (and they elect only 100 Senators and 435 Representatives). When you consider that elections are now won or lost in a few marginal constituencies it becomes clear that, as a system to involve people, our democracy is little more than a charade.

Nothing much in the democratic system has changed in over a hundred years and yet the same basic model has to cope with many, many more people whose voices have an equal right to be heard. And, because there are many, many more people with many more options, the task of holding society together *within* the existing framework has become infinitely more complicated. The number of decisions that government now feels it needs to take, and is asked to take, on our behalf continues to grow without any change in the means to do it. It is like expecting Stephenson's *Rocket* to pull a high-speed train and, not surprisingly, it is struggling. Those hundred or more years have also seen expectations rise as the result of better education and less deferential attitudes, yet opportunities for meaningful participation in the political process have actually declined.

Democracy, if it is to work effectively, however, is about more than the number of votes cast. It should be a conversation between those represented and their representatives, a ongoing feedback loop that ensures that the social magnet remains charged and continues to provide an overall sense of direction and purpose. Feedback, as we have seen, is also about ensuring that issues are tackled before they become major problems. Thus, government is about allowing people to contribute to their community and for that to feel as natural as breathing. It should release energy rather than tie it down by being both facilitator and listener. The political process should alternately lead and allow itself to be led, both articulating what people may be unconsciously thinking and feeling, and having the humility to leave well alone.

In reality, the opposite is happening. To cope with the increase in business that our ever-more complex world produces, governments have not only tended to become more centralised, they have spawned vast bureaucracies to codify and implement the decisions of those in power (in 2004 the public sector employed around seven million people in the UK[2]). Language is important and, although governments are always careful to emphasise their role as public servants, the reality often breaks through as in the use of phrases such as 'European Directives' used to describe the regulations produced in Brussels on behalf of the European Union; directives is exactly what they are, sets of rules to be disseminated and effected in each of the member states, so that people from Plymouth to Prague, from Stockholm to Seville are brought under the same umbrella and deemed to see the world through the same eyes. President De Gaulle of France (1890-1970) once despaired of being able to govern a country with 246 different, local cheeses[3]: we no longer appear to believe this to be an issue.

It is a purely imperialistic impulse. The Emperor Napoleon (1769-1821), for example, did something similar and, if his standardisation of the legal and metric systems in Europe was largely successful, it was because he lived in a simpler world. Today the bureaucracies necessary to produce conformity and compliance are not only larger, they cover almost every aspect of human activity from child care to food preparation, from employment practice to land use. Much of what was previously considered private has been brought into the public domain. In the process, hierarchical mini-empires have been created who see themselves as the guardians of their particular brand of truth, which they not only have to implement rigorously but defend (and justify) against the other mini-empires who have very different missions, agendas, planning cycles and priorities. This ongoing battle for status and funding is a breeding ground for blinkered thinking, and encourages closed systems of decision-making where the focus on a narrow aspect of reality frees the exponents from the constraints of the wider picture, or of responsibility for their impact on the wider world.

Alexis de Tocqueville (1805-1859) summed it up over a hundred and fifty years ago when he warned of the despotism inherent in democracy – "It covers the surface of society with a network of small complicated rules, minute and uniform, through which the most original minds and the most energetic characters cannot penetrate, to rise above the crowd. The will of man is not shattered, but softened, bent, and guided; men are seldom forced by it to act, but they are constantly restrained from acting: such a power does not destroy, but it prevents existence; it does not tyrannize, but it compresses, enervates, extinguishes, and stupefies a people, till each nation is reduced to be nothing better than a flock of timid and industrious animals, of which the government is the shepherd"[4].

The Great and the Good – Public Servants All

The basic democratic process may be little different to that of a hundred years ago, but the political landscape against which elections are played out has changed beyond recognition. Nowhere is that more apparent than in the process by which American presidents gain power. A cornerstone of the American Dream is the belief that anyone can become President and, at the outset, that dream probably came closer to reality than most. Today, the race for the White House is between career politicians who fight for institutional support to fund their campaigns (even Clinton (born 1943), from the humblest of beginnings in Hope, Arkansas, was a political insider with years of building the momentum necessary for that final assault on the summit of power).

Politics in the USA, as elsewhere, has always been a dirty business, but the deals that are necessary today have less and less to do with real people and more to do with balancing the interests of the power brokers behind the scenes with the need to present attractive, vote-winning campaigns, centred on artificially constructed and manipulated public personae. It is an essentially tribal way of electing a leader and it is expected that the spoils will go to the successful candidate's immediate family (that today is a family of interest). Democracy is the fig-leaf that gives the process decency and, in so doing, becomes its greatest casualty. All power structures (whether political, corporate, military or religious) isolate and insulate the great and the good from the effects of their decisions, providing explanations that usually centre on some "greater good". They become closed systems, seeing only what they want to see, and increasingly ignoring the individuals who have given them power. What America does today, Britain does tomorrow and Europe the day after: the signs are that the trend is well advanced throughout the Western world.

The very process that should engage our hearts and minds, that should reflect both our hopes and uncertainties about what makes life worth living, has become a fortress from which we are effectively barred. To take the fortress analogy a step further, life today for those of us outside the walls (the excluded) is akin to that of a medieval peasant, forced to pay our feudal dues (taxes) and prey to any robber baron (the institutional world) whose path we cross. Protection has always been the prerogative of the powerful, and the fact that we, as individuals, increasingly need protection from the big battalions that surround us demonstrates just how powerless we are.

It is all a far cry from a concept of democracy rooted in the Greek polis where those eligible gathered in the marketplace, listened and contributed to the arguments and then placed their counters in one of two earthenware jars (for and against). They were debating matters of immediate import and, although voting was undoubtedly divided along family or other lines on many issues, opinions could be changed and consensus achieved. Equally important, decisions once taken could be reviewed in the light of experience (feedback) and other options considered.

An impossible ideal in this day and age, where voter numbers run into millions and the pace of life is fast and complicated; where we need the advice of specialists (another example of closed systems – focusing on ever narrower fields of view and ignoring everything outside) just to keep on top of change and development? Not so. There remains one Western society that has managed to buck the trend of democratic dilution and that is Switzerland, a highly stable (dating back to 1291), decentralised state with a population of 7.45 million (2.8 million in 1880) that is wealthy, technologically advanced and manages to embrace four different languages and cultures (German, French, Italian and Romansch)[5]. Divided into twenty-six cantons and further subdivided into communes (each a mini local authority), there is considerable autonomy at the very local level with villagers and townspeople coming together to allocate education, welfare and road building budgets (some cantons still hold open-air parliaments each spring).

Co-operation on larger-scale projects such as highways, water, electricity and other infrastructure requirements is nevertheless good, as the reputation of Swiss railways attests. But the centre never intrudes. Many Swiss do not know which of the seven elected Federal Councillors is acting as President (chosen by the others as primus inter pares) and, until security was tightened following a shooting at the regional parliament building of Zug in 2001, in which fourteen elected representatives were killed, open access to the national and regional parliaments was an absolute right for all citizens.

Meaningful participation is possible in today's world but the odds are increasingly stacked against it. The focus in most so-called mature democracies is not on the direct participation of the electorate in the issues that effect them but on the increasingly symbolic act of casting their vote. And that is because of the adversarial nature of the political process in most of the Western world. On a regular, if infrequent basis, the public is asked to choose from a list of candidates distinguished only by their party allegiance (in some instances, such as elections for Members of the European Parliament, voting is for a party rather than a candidate). Candidates themselves often have only tenuous links with the localities they seek to represent, are selected by a tiny minority of the community (party activists) and yet they are supposed to speak for their constituents.

In most cases, differences between parties are reflected in vague manifestos that few voters are likely to wholeheartedly endorse in their entirety. By voting for a particular candidate we are effectively signing up to a package that may bear little relation to the words and phrases that attracted us in the first place. Likewise, we can't know whether our particular priorities are shared by the party of our choice (which are likely to change with access to power anyway).

Few people today feel they are truly represented by the system, which is another symptom of the atomistic nature of our societies. Although politicians work frenetically during the run-up to an election trying to align the people behind them, no charge results from the process and the whole thing is forgotten as soon as it is over. From beginning to end, our electoral systems are hardly a recipe for grown-up decision-making.

The growth in single-issue politics – an individual or party asking people to vote for them on the basis of a commitment to end or endorse one, and only one, star in the political firmament – is the logical response to this lack of real choice: it nevertheless equally distorts a process whose objective is to provide a government that is capable of responding to the wide range of issues that it will face in a way that is likely to be generally supported by the population at large. It is, however, a sign of the worrying sense of disenfranchisement that pervades politics today and represents the last stop along a road that leads to anarchy and violence on the one hand or ever more repression on the other.

To compensate for the inadequacy of the electoral system as an indication of what is actually important to people, all political parties now routinely take soundings through focus groups and surveys to try to establish what public opinion feels about issues – a process that becomes increasingly feverish as election time approaches. And therein lies the clue to the fact that the system is no longer truly adversarial but conceals an ongoing battle for the middle ground; a ceaseless and edgy contest to catch and reflect the public mood. Parties are branded to give the illusion

45

of serious choice and small differences are hyped to create the impression that 'clear blue water' exists between policies that are essentially the same (in the UK, for example, much is made about who will control public spending and deliver efficient services – the reality is that only a couple of percentage points separate the two major parties on a spend that represents around 50% of GDP). Once successfully positioned and secure in the knowledge that it is on-trend, a party in power is then free to pursue its own priorities or those determined by the political realities of the global marketplace.

All the surveys indicate that what concerns the public remains remarkably stable over time – fear of crime, worry over health services and a desire for clean streets – and has little to do with reality on the ground so, even if crime is falling, there has to be a continual emphasis on being tough on crime. There *is* concern over the environment but it is not sufficiently strong, as yet, for that to appear in the priorities that the major political parties reflect back to the electorate at election time – which is why green parties across the world struggle to escape from the political shadows. A system that can't even get the biggest challenge we currently face on the agenda must be suspect and reflects the reality that elections are a necessary evil to those in power, and winning them is essentially a reactive, damage limitation exercise that depends more on PR than policy, and more on image than content.

This preoccupation with presentation masks an absence of any new political ideas or ideology. No political party that sees itself as having a realistic chance of being elected has a commitment to anything other than maintaining the status quo, i.e. the onward march of the global economy. That is why the threat of terrorism has been such a godsend to the political elite. They no longer have to create the fiction that they, and they alone, can deliver on health, wealth and happiness. All they now have to do is promise to protect us, to stand firm and resolute in the face of an unspecified menace. They've been given a licence to do whatever they want – and they don't even have to tell people. It's being done in the name of liberty and democracy, so what's your problem?

You don't have to search far to understand why we have this uneasy relationship with the concept of democracy and why so much of what happens in practice is more akin to the workings of empire. We are the inheritors. When your civilisation enjoys the position of top dog, and when your need for bread and circuses is being met, your critical faculties tend to be dulled. It is natural to assume that there is not only merit in your way of life, but that you have a duty to let the world know that, if only they were as virtuous as you, they too could enjoy the good life. Except that they never can in reality, because your good fortune usually depends on them being kept in their place. And, if you want to know what happens to such systems when they face serious challenges, look no further than the decline and fall of Rome.

If You're Not For Me, You Must be Against Me

How have we reached this state of affairs? The evolution of adversarial politics of the eighteenth and nineteenth centuries changed the political landscape because issues were split largely along lines that were evident to all (enfranchised-disenfranchised, landowners-landless, employers-employees, town-country, rich-poor). Often violent protests at home and revolutions elsewhere focused the minds of the ruling elites and produced the tension between conservatives and progressives that could lead to dramatic change. Once the genie was out of the bottle and universal suffrage had been achieved, however, rising living standards, increased mobility and a diminishing identification with local communities combined to produce a general sense that our number one priority was ourselves. The kind of seismic fault lines over which previous generations had struggled gradually dissolved and, with their disappearance, the radical political stances that could produce genuine alternatives were no longer tenable. In any case, the globalisation of the marketplace described in the previous chapter has increasingly imposed an economic straitjacket on governments that leaves them very little room for manoeuvre, whatever the colour of their letterhead and slogans; when an individual is in debt their options are limited, it is no different when every nation, the whole world, is up to their ears in it.

47

In these circumstances it might be thought that consensus would become the norm and that politicians would acknowledge the situation they find themselves in. But they are slaves to the system that has given them prominence, and the adversarial nature of the political system they have inherited means that those in power want to hold on to it while those in opposition want their turn in the sun. All conspire to present government as a series of watershed decisions that only they have the vision and moral stature to take. Sound bite and spin have replaced debate and the kind of informed discussion that might lead to the establishment of common ground. Politics has become a self-contained, closed system.

Worse still, so used are we to a political landscape of adversaries locked in battle for the ultimate prize that those who might be termed progressives (who do see an alternative to the current headlong rush towards disaster) embrace adversarial politics as if it were the natural order. Because they are effectively excluded from power, they tend to become ever more extreme and to define themselves as opposed, not so much to the existing power structure (which is taken as read – although there is an ongoing conflict between wanting to destroy it and a sneaking desire to get their hands on the levers of government), but to other groups of progressives who they define as reactionary or degenerate.

Small and often incidental aspects of an opponent's agenda can lead to irreparable schism. In Germany, green politics has divided along left and conservative lines, the former supporting gay rights, the latter standing for traditional family values. The fact that these issues are not mutually exclusive does not prevent people, who should be uniting around core issues of sustainability, weakening their impact through largely artificial divisions[6]. Real hatred can be generated in these destructive bouts of bloodletting and, by a strange inversion, groups can take on the characteristics of those they demonise. The most obvious example is the violent pacifist or anti-war demonstrator who thinks nothing of wrecking property and throwing missiles to injure and maim the police who are sent against them. Aggression replaces argument and is the more easily dealt with by the powers that be as a consequence. Most people want only to be left in peace and will support any measures that remove what they perceive to be a threat to their security.

The lack of a credible alternative to mainstream politics leads directly to the frustration and apathy that is such a feature of Western democracy. Coupled with an absence of transparency about what government is doing, this sense of being disempowered fuels conspiracy theories – from the death of Princess Diana to US involvement in 9/11 – and further erodes the legitimacy of the electoral systems. Governments now rule through a mixture of voter indifference and their power to mobilise the big battalions to enforce their will when necessary. In short, adversarial politics has had its day. Either our political institutions shed their pretence to be democratic – moving inevitably in the direction of a de facto world government dominated by Western priorities and values – or they re-evaluate the democratic ideal that supposedly underpins our most cherished beliefs about our civilisation. Do we as individuals matter, or not? It's as stark as that.

Are Cities the New Nations?

From around the twelfth century the history of Western Europe (and thus the world) has been a gradual consolidation of the continent into a network of sovereign nation states whose boundaries were recognised, if not always respected, by a series of mutual treaties. In the rush to dismember empire that followed the Second World War, lines were drawn on maps and states created that mirrored the experience of the West. By the end of the twentieth century there wasn't anywhere on the Earth that wasn't encompassed by nationhood and, in 2005, 193 countries proudly displayed their flags at the United Nations (up from 51 in 1945), and were promised the protection of international law in return. You could be forgiven for thinking that the era of the nation, as the basic building block of the global fabric, was firmly established.

You would be wrong. The nation state today is looking decidedly shaky and in many instances has already become an irrelevance. On the one hand, it is under attack from the unrelenting logic of globalisation and the powerful corporations that are struggling to dominate and exploit markets everywhere: on the other, from the attempt to "localise" (while still retaining central control, an interesting balancing act!) as the latest buzz word in the increasingly desperate search for a way to reverse the ossification of the body politic described above. A third threat is also evident in the form of an increasing number of independence and secessionist movements seeking autonomy for geographical areas within existing states: there are active separatist movements in some two dozen nations around the globe, including some twenty-eight within the United States alone[7].

But the most serious menace to the pre-eminence of the nation state is likely to come from an unexpected source – the rise of cities as the basic unit in the struggle to claim a share of the global spoils. It has been estimated that, by 2010, 51% of the global population of around eight billion will live in cities[8] (with in excess of two billion living in squatter communities by 2030, approximately one person in four[9]) and that there will be over five hundred cities with populations of a million plus[10] (implying an additional three hundred cities growing from smaller, existing entities over the next ten years). Already cities are vying with each other to brand themselves as centres of enterprise, providing the infrastructure and service needs that any corporate giant might need, coupled with an easily accessible pool of skilled and unskilled labour. The aim is simple, to remain competitive in an increasingly cutthroat, global marketplace.

The evidence suggests that cities with strong leadership (usually in the form of a long-term, elected mayor acting as chief executive) are beginning to win the race, creating business-friendly forms of governance that can create effective public-private partnerships. Indeed, what might be called the creditworthiness of cities and their ability to commit for the long haul is becoming a significant consideration: in other words, how far a city can insulate itself from the vagaries of national and international politics. In response, cities are taking on the panoply of mini-states, putting up futuristic, iconic buildings – galleries, theatres, stadia and international airports – on a scale that would once have been the preserve of a capital city and a reflection of national enterprise. Such state-of-the-art architecture has little to do with the city itself, its history and heritage, and everything to do with branding, ensuring that it is easily distinguishable from its competitors. It will not be long before cities look to take on some of the legislative functions that have hitherto resided with central government and effectively become responsible for their own destinies. The nation state is unlikely to be able to withstand such pressures for long.

Shouldn't we be applauding such a trend? With an electorate of only a million plus rather than the fifty, one hundred or two hundred million that make up nations, surely the chance of having a representative democracy that truly reflects the wishes of the people becomes possible again? For the visionaries there is the prospect of technological democracy, where every house on an estate or neighbourhood is connected to a central computer and individuals can comment on how their services are being provided at the click of a mouse, and respond to questionnaires drafted by management committees to ascertain the preferences of the majority.

Consultation it may be, but increased democratisation it is not. We are so used to democracy being about putting our cross in a box (or pressing a button on a computer) that we have forgotten that true democracy is what happened in the town squares in Greece two thousand four hundred years ago, where people were actively engaged in, and exposed to, different points of view so that, when they voted, they had thought through the issues. The kind of continuous polling that is being proposed is a means of smoothing the management process by creating the illusion of involvement; it is at one with the couch potato's dream of never having to get off their butts or use their brains.

Certainly governance will potentially be more effective and responsive to both internal and external changes at the city level, but remember that this new breed of cities will be in many ways indistinguishable from the vast corporations they are trying to woo and the meeting of whose needs will be their number one priority. A business that runs a factory knows that it has to provide facilities that meet certain standards (although those are often negotiable or simply neglected when competition is fierce). Employees should work in a clean, welcoming environment, they need access to wash rooms, dining areas, etc., and they need to be trained and motivated. That will increasingly be the perspective taken in the new cities in relation to their inhabitants. It will not be about responding to people's hopes and fears, but a means of keeping the lid on things. After all, only cities that look good and convey a sense of energy and vitality will be the winners in the new world order. Another closed system, pursuing a single goal and ignoring everything else, will have been created.

In fact, it's already happening. Economic development and regeneration of run-down neighbourhoods are flavour of the month (a tacit admission that previous, centrally controlled policies have produced large areas of deprivation). New legions of officials are being brought together to try and reverse the trend by creating partnerships that include government departments at local, regional and nation level, as well as involving the private and voluntary sectors. "Sustainable Communities" is the new catchphrase. Decoded, it simply means the creation of neighbourhoods that are clean and safe, where people want to live, where house prices continue to rise as a result, and where the inhabitants are so grateful that they will vote for the party who has given them this paradise for evermore.

The approach doesn't even pay lip service to sustainability in the sense in which it has been defined earlier (or even to community in the sense of local empowerment and involvement in the decision-making processes). Rather than being about real people, it is a way of looking at the urban landscape as a whole, a shorthand to provide the officials and developers charged with regenerating (or creating) whole communities, towns and even cities with a sense of purpose and justification. The aim is to provide an environment that will be attractive to business as being the only way to guarantee the long-term future of an area.

And there, as they say, is the rub. For every city that succeeds there will be many that fail and you only have to look at cities in the developing world to realise the implications for those who fall by the wayside. Shantytowns and open sewers may yet become commonplace in the heartlands of the wealthy West.

Traditionally cities have lived off their hinterlands and their expansion in terms of population has been limited by the ability of the surrounding countryside to provide the necessities of life. It was a symbiotic relationship with the city providing wealth and manufactured goods in exchange for produce, and the countryside was always a visible presence in towns and cities in terms of animals being driven to market. That affinity has long since disappeared as food travels up and down the country and is flown in from all over the world.

City dwellers no longer have a direct link with the way their food is produced and casually assume that it will always be available on the supermarket shelves. The new-style cities will see themselves as sovereign entities with no relationship with their hinterlands. They will grow according to their ability to create the wealth necessary to transport in whatever needs their citizens might have – which is why the consequences of failure will be so profound; the money to buy in goods and services will have gone and the surrounding countryside won't be structured to support (it will be orientated to wider markets), or necessarily be capable of supporting, the size of population that the city has grown to. When some of the implications of the challenges we face really begin to bite – particularly the increasing scarcity of oil and its by-products – living in cities as currently structured could become very unpleasant and uncomfortable indeed.

In summary, the future is there on the horizon and it doesn't work. Our political system – which should be shaping the human agenda – has simply run out of ideas. It came into being in a different era as a response to a very different reality. It is an anachronism that keeps going only because it keeps going. There is no longer the grit within that might even produce the pearl of true change. It has become a closed system that has lost the ability to re-invent itself. Worse still, its sheer size has produced an arthritic inflexibility that compounds the very problems it is trying to ameliorate, producing simplistic responses to complex issues. The continually expanding and bureaucratic, hierarchical nature of the agencies that government deploys to interpret its policies in practice leads to inflexibility and confusion on the ground. Competition for resources and status means that the kind of co-operation necessary to effect real change is the exception rather than the rule; time, energy and resources all disappear into the sand. And beneath it all, the system's very inability to respond to the problems it faces allows imperial ambitions full rein. In terms of rising to the challenges we have identified we can expect little from such a closed system.

Put simply the whole thing is just too big and complicated to meet the changing needs of real people – the basic rationale for its existence. Central government may see its role as enabling, but its essentially top-down orientation means that it can only ever see the big picture and make broad-brush responses. By contrast, looking from the ground up, ordinary people can usually see a whole range of answers to their problems, if only they had the opportunity to do something about them. As isolated individuals, however, we have long since handed over responsibility to the vast and unwieldy systems of governance in the belief that it will allow us to get on with our own private interests unfettered by the needs of others. It is no good complaining when the system doesn't meet our needs because it doesn't meet anybody's.

A Divine Right of Kings Moment demands that we face up to the fact that our political system doesn't have the answer to the problems we face – in fact, it compounds them. Just because something has been around for a long time doesn't mean it has some absolute right to continue. The rule of kings gave way to the rule of parliaments. It is now time for the rule of parliaments to give way to something else.

At the end of the day, it is the decisions that we as individuals make that will determine what tomorrow will actually bring. What opportunities are there for us to stand aside from the blind rush of "progress" and create something different, something that might compensate for the inability of government at whatever level to confront the gathering storm clouds? To answer that question we need to look at the forms of civil society available to us.

4

No Such Thing as Society?

If the governance systems as represented by the economy and politics have now become closed, so large that they no longer reflect the needs of real people, imperialistic in nature and inextricably tied to the headlong dash towards an ever more unsustainable future, what is left? What if anything can we, as individuals and communities, do to turn back the tide? We are after all social beings with the capacity to make choices and co-operate in achieving them. In theory at least, we should be capable of acting individually and collectively in a way that will make a difference.

The British Prime Minister Margaret Thatcher (born 1925) once famously remarked that "there is no such thing as society: there are individual men and women and there are families"[1]. She went on to say, "no government can do anything except through the people, and people must look to themselves first". It was a call for the kind of rugged individualism that is more usually associated with the United States, but it chimed with the times, perfectly capturing the rootless, go-getting individualism that distinguished the 1980s and a Britain in transition. It was suddenly all right to look after Number One and it didn't matter too much how you got on as long as you did. Life had become a jungle and you had to struggle to come out on top.

Was she right? In terms of the kind of mass culture that passes for society today she had a point. Looked at from a distance, society today presents a totally institutional landscape, a bewildering, brightly coloured array of logos, branding and mission statements that continually shout their wares in an attempt to drown out the voice of the competition. It is a world characterised by ceaseless movement, activity and speed; technology, street upon street of office blocks, the ritual of rush-hour migration, all create a rhythm that dominates life and makes it hard to imagine any other reality. Although people are part of this vast abstraction they only come together for a narrowly defined purpose and they are ultimately expendable. People take the institution into themselves – it becomes part of their meaning structure – but the institution never takes the individual into itself.

Put that another way round: institutions influence the way people think and act, people rarely influence institutions in the same way; institutions follow a logic and an agenda entirely their own, to which people conform or are thrown out.

When we fall foul of this depersonalised world whether as employee, consumer, customer, client or patient there is little option but to turn to another institutional body in the form of the various official watchdogs and regulatory bodies who now police daily life. Other options include taking court action or going to the papers, but not one of these alternatives is concerned with the actual person who appears before them, only in whether their problem fits in with their *brief*, allowing them to exercise their power and justify their existence.

They are not interested in the human detail, the complexity of individual cases; all must be sorted according to some pre-existent categorisation that will indicate whether success (in the institution's terms) is likely or not. If not, we will be politely but firmly shown the door and, even when a case is proven, we are unlikely to be entirely satisfied with the outcome (the institution may have notched up another success, but compensation or apologies rarely satisfy the our basic human need for closure, which is having our injury acknowledged in the fullest sense). And with the frustration and hurt caused by institutional practice becoming almost a daily occurrence in our lives, we are getting inured to it and can find the energy to complain only in extreme cases. In this environment, it is questionable today whether we can even look to ourselves.

Most of us are not going to be able to use the positions we occupy in the institutional world (whether as employees, consumers or victims) to change its agenda, even though we all spend most of our lives dancing to its tune in one form or another. That does not mean that corporations and public institutions won't respond to changes in consciousness about the importance of living sustainably. They are, after all, in the business of moulding and manipulating public perception and taste, and their antennae are finely tuned. They will, however, interpret that concern from their own limited perspectives, make largely cosmetic changes and carry on as normal. Already, adopting 'green' and 'natural' credentials has become a feature of advertising campaigns for products as diverse as cars and shampoo. With energy prices set to rise there will undoubtedly be a switch to investment in renewable forms of energy, but the basic nature of the animal – and its destructive impact on human life – will remain essentially unchanged.

The problem with such a world is that it isn't human. People are sucked dry in pursuit of goals that, in the grand scheme of things, aren't very important. Huge amounts of energy, creativity and emotion are consumed by institutions, but they are invariably directed towards an end that is unworthy of the time, talent and resources being expended. Does it really take hundreds of people spread across the world to produce, market and sell an item of fashion wear that will be thrown away in a couple of months? And as organisations get bigger most of the effort goes in just keeping them functioning. We have created monsters that are slowly devouring us. A Divine Right of Kings Moment should remind us that these are purely human constructs and there is nothing god-given about them. They can and should be removed.

Meanwhile, Back in the Trenches

So, is there no glimmer of hope on the horizon? Well, fortunately, real life continues to exist beneath the radar of the big battalions - just. It is called civil society, and is the crucial ingredient that Margaret Thatcher left out of her analysis, probably because she wasn't aware of its existence and had never contributed to it. Civil society is the coming together of real people in their daily round of living, to share in and support one another's ups and down, joys and sorrows. It is based on the assumption that people are generally reasonable, helpful and decent and will continue to be so.

The premise of civil society can be summed up in the desert philosophy: I will offer you help and hospitality today because, tomorrow, I might require it from you. In a hostile environment little distinction is made between neighbours and strangers and there are still a few isolated places in the world where, poor as the people may be (particularly when compared with the almost obscene wealth that is everywhere on display in the West), hospitality is viewed as a sacred duty. Strangers are welcomed in and urged to share what food and shelter is available. Such identification with the other is almost inconceivable in our society, if only because the number of people who pass through our lives on a daily basis effectively prohibits it. We offer hospitality, if and when we do, to those we know or those we wish to get to know, influence or impress.

It is a controlled, selfish reaching out and we are the poorer for it because, once the bonds of mutual obligation begin to unravel, so much of what makes civil society vibrant and valuable gradually ebbs away and, in our hour of need, we are likely to be left to face the harsh reality of life alone. We have become a society not so much of strangers, as of self-contained atoms moving around and interacting in the kind of random, meaningless patterns that leaves the social magnet without charge, lifeless and lacking the power to effect anything within its field.

Traditionally civil society provided the buffer between the individual and a frequently hostile and indifferent external world. From the dawn of human history groups defined along tribal, cultural or religious lines have looked after their own. There is evidence that the earliest hunter-gatherers cared for the weak even though they represented no economic benefit to the group. Incidents such as a child drowning in a lake surrounded by picnickers enjoying a sunny day in the park, or commuters walking past someone who has collapsed on the street, demonstrate that we cannot take this inbuilt compassion and identification with the plight of others for granted. In mass society particularly it can quickly become an endangered species.

Rather amazingly, and encouragingly given what institutions do to us, people still try to reach out to one another and connect, whether as co-workers or in making contact with the wider world on behalf of their organisation. In fact, work has become one of the few opportunities left for ongoing association, providing a measure of continuity in our fractured lives and we seize it enthusiastically. But then, the same thing happens in prisons, mental hospitals and concentration camps. We are social creatures with a need to express that side of ourselves no matter how discouraging the circumstances.

As an indication of how central work now is to satisfying our need for association with others, women who leave to have children find themselves vegetating and feeling devalued, and yearn to return. They have lost a vital bit of their identity and have nothing to replace it with. Even if a mother doesn't have to go back to work for purely economic reasons, she is likely to worry that she is missing out in career terms, or simply that she is not using her brain and talents to good effect. Given that most work actually isn't that demanding, this fear suggests that child care is neither seen as work nor considered to be important in itself. Until we redefine the concept of work to embrace both paid and unpaid activity and discover ways in which the bringing up of children can be reintegrated into mainstream life (as it always has been), we are in effect denying the natural cycles of life and death. The institutional world is like a machine; when a part breaks you throw it away and replace it. It is as simple as that, only the parts happen to be human beings.

Maybe this dehumanising aspect of institutional work wouldn't be so bad if it hadn't become so central to our social lives. Sadly, it is now provides most people with their sole opportunity to experience and participate in civil society. At the local, neighbourhood level, traditional forms of association provided by the Church, local shops and other amenities, clubs and self-help groups have gradually disappeared to be replaced, if at all, by larger-scale, organised volunteering along specialised lines (age, handicap, illness, etc.) or interest groups that may have a membership that is spread across the world, courtesy of the internet. Neighbours keep themselves to themselves and there are few opportunities to influence things that happen in one's own street, let alone the immediate neighbourhood. Schools have grown larger and become increasingly insitutionalised, having to follow procedures, to perform and produce results, determined by a distant local or central government, so the impact that individual parents can have is diminished to the point of exclusion. It is not fertile ground within which the seeds of change might be sown.

Historically speaking, civil society has not had a good press, being portrayed as oppressive and reactionary. All such association is a trade-off between the benefits of being part of something greater than yourself and the burden of having to conform to certain expectations. At its worst, it becomes a tyranny, allowing one section of society to impose its will and priorities on others. Patriarchy can be seen in this way, exacting a severe curtailment in the liberty of women as the price for the protection of the family or tribe. We may wonder at how women accepted enforced marriage, beatings and a life of back-breaking drudgery for so long, but it is really no different from the many examples of Divine Right of Kings Moments that we have been discussing in relation to our own era – something has been going on for so long that it appears to be self-evidently right and we don't even bother to question it; that is just the way things are and there appears to be no obvious alternative.

Like all human constructs, civil society is a reflection of the individuals who compose it at any given time. Each generation has to interpret and re-interpret what they have been handed by their parents and therein lies both the opportunity and the danger. If civil society is to be anything other than the dead hand of habit and tradition, usually anchoring and justifying existing power and privilege relations, it has to be capable of renewing and re-inventing itself. In other words, it doesn't have to be a backward-looking, reactionary force, it can become the main motor for real change – as happened during the Industrial Revolution.

At its best, civil society offers that most precious of experiences, the identification of self with others through bonds of mutual love and support in the furtherance of a shared vision or goal; it gives life meaning, in short. With our quick fix, have-it-all-now mentality and emphasis on me, me, me, that possibility doesn't even register. We are so afraid of being constrained, of having to conform, that we have lost sight of the simple truth that there is no such thing as a free lunch in this life. Seeking something for nothing does damage to the intricate web of interrelationships that characterises reality. Everything effects everything else: what happens here has an impact there. To take without giving ruptures the symmetry that civil society, in its concern for neighbours and strangers, is striving to maintain; the balance between the needs of the self and other. And once that has goe, it really is a return to law of the jungle.

Going Backwards into the Future

We have not reached that sorry state quite yet and it is worth going back in time and asking how we have come to the point where we can even contemplate the demise of civil society, let alone view its potential disappearance with such complacency. All the earliest forms of association were based on the family and immediate community, defined in terms of blood, religion or custom, and complex systems to support those unable to look after themselves evolved. From their earliest days, the Jews, for example, saw contributing towards the welfare of the community as central to their religion; charity was the same word as righteous. Wealth was redistributed through the synagogue that rich and poor alike attended, with different funds providing food and clothes for widows, the poor, aged and sick, as well schooling and burial for those unable to afford them: as many as one family in five was supported in this way. Such systems evolved to include individuals with similar interests, as can be seen in the example of the medieval city guilds, which offered a mutual insurance scheme to protect oneself and one's family from the vagaries of existence.

These early social structures were based on face-to-face relationships. People knew each other and, recognising the connections that existed between them (husband-wife, father-daughter, aunt-niece), understood the obligations that this entailed. Those bonds continue (a daughter is likely to turn to her own mother when she is about to give birth to her first child), although their effectiveness has been much reduced by distance and the existence of welfare agencies, and they do not sit altogether easily with today's impersonal, meritocratic world where work is the dominant expression of self-worth and a reflection of personal achievement rather than family connection.

In large parts of Africa, for example, the sense of family obligation that those who succeed in business or government office feel towards their family can be seen as problematic in the West[2]. The expectation is that successful individuals will share their good fortune by securing jobs for relatives and distributing any financial rewards in other ways. We see it as corruption, but it is really an unwillingness to fully make the transition from personal to impersonal obligation; from direct involvement with our kith and kin (and possibly strangers) to the paying of taxes in lieu of this service so that others might do it on our behalf. This reluctance is also reflected in the way that most Africans are not fully individualised in the Western sense, but continue to see their identity as tied up with their family and tribal relationships; they are more likely to talk of 'we' than of 'I'. They instinctively recognise what they are losing, while we, who have forgotten we ever had it, respond only with frustration.

Several aspects of the journey that the West has taken, particularly in the past two hundred and fifty years, begin to come into focus. First, we have become individualised; we have ceased to define ourselves in terms of a web of mutual relationships. We refer loosely to our friends and family almost as if they were interchangeable and, if we have to move around the world in pursuit of our career, that is exactly what they become; we constantly have to reinvent our social networks. In our struggle to gain individual liberty by throwing off the shackles of a social order based on birth, position and gender, we have become suspicious of any call on our time and resources, whether emotional or financial, that is based on another's relationship to us; we, in turn, try to avoid becoming indebted to others. Individualistic effort is the way we prove our worth to wider society. Any advancement we receive should be through merit rather than connection.

Second, the rewards for our individualistic endeavour have come to be measured solely in terms of money and/or power (the two are usually closely linked). Third, the money and power that come with success are now related directly to performance in the money economy (rather than to more abstract notions of contributing to human well-being or happiness) and, fourthly, to be able to divert the maximum amount of available energy into the economic sphere, the role of mutual obligation in caring for society's casualties has been squeezed to the margins and replaced with institutional systems of welfare.

As a process, it didn't happen overnight, it wasn't planned and the end result we see today wasn't inevitable. The key event was rapid and continuing urbanisation. To fuel the Industrial Revolution in Britain, for example, raw labour was needed in unprecedented quantities and new towns and cities exploded into being. Rural poverty meant there were also strong push factors and the sudden tide of people leaving the countryside stretched and eroded old loyalties to breaking point. New working patterns in the mills and manufactories left little time and energy for mutual support (although, as novels such as *North and South*[3] suggest, the impulse wasn't entirely eradicated) and placed a new emphasis on the nuclear family as the unit to which individuals clung.

Conditions in the second half of the nineteenth century in Britain, then the greatest industrial power in the world, were dire and widely reported through the works of the Victorian novelists and such classics as Charles Booth's *Life and Labour of the People in London*[4]. In these circumstances it is perhaps not surprising that the greatest source of social welfare (schools, hospitals, friendly societies, etc.) came from local (usually very local) voluntary associations. It was as if the shock of what had happened, the tangible wrench with the past, had brought people together to fill the void that government was unable or unwilling to fill. A rich, if uneven, tapestry of personal commitment to the needs of others (strangers) came into being.

Even as this very human response to need was growing, so worldwide competition for markets intensified and the ongoing need to keep prices down led to ever-bigger factories, dwarfing individuals and their ability to have any control over their situation. In these circumstances, trades unions came increasingly to the fore and with them the notion of collective action around specific issues (as opposed to family support that was available across the full spectrum of life's ups and downs). Society became ever more polarised along class lines and this new power base of the unions created the impetus towards a political identification with the needs of the working classes seen in terms of their general working and living conditions rather than the importance of individual family or community ties. Communism, socialism and social democracy share the same roots and, as a political force, began to make their presence felt on the world stage, particularly after the First World War had swept away a generation of Europeans and Americans and, with them, old certainties about society and the individual's place within it.

As the population grew and suburbia began to sprawl, so the ability of individuals and groups to respond to even local need diminished and people looked increasingly to local and central government for solutions. On both sides of the Atlantic, the Great Depression was a seminal moment, leading directly to government intervention to create the conditions for continuing employment and economic growth. World War Two confirmed the trend towards increasing centralisation of the national effort and, in Britain at least, the experience led to the creation of the welfare state.

Now that government was finally and clearly centre stage, the instinct, common to all political parties, was to want to stay there, to standardise, monitor and control. The creation of the National Health Service swept away, at a stroke, the network of private, charitable and voluntary institutions that had been evolving since the Middle Ages, replacing them with one-size-fits-all approach to health care. Local boards gave an element of local control, but the mere fact that the new service was directly answerable to government meant it evolved as a top-down, bureaucratically accountable machine.

Without stretching credulity too much, this transfer of functions from the human and engaged to the objective and detached can be seen as a transfer from the feminine to the masculine. This continuation of paternalistic priorities – control, order, hierarchy – under the guise of freedom and democracy mirrors the way empire now operates behind the cloak of the free market; in fact, the triumph of the masculine characterises the changes that we have seen in all the areas we have considered. Paternalism has been supplanted only in the sense that now women as well as men have an equal opportunity to act in destructive and dehumanising ways for their own immediate gain and benefit, and other people – men as well as women – have to suffer as a consequence.

Another unintended consequence of the taking over of welfare by central government has been to bring the system finally and irrevocably into the money economy. That trend is evident in every aspect of life, but it has been particularly disastrous in an area that had hitherto been largely undertaken by civil society. Humans constantly do things for one another without thinking about whether the compliment will be returned; such activity provides a sense of competence, of being needed and of being involved. It is a system of exchange that depends on values that have nothing to do money. As soon as payment and the notion of a fair return enter the equation, however, the impulse to help becomes a calculation. As more and more functions can only be obtained for cash (from simple repairs to organising social activities) what we do for each other becomes increasingly trivial. Not only is the social fabric poorer as a consequence, we are becoming de-skilled, having to find and pay for assistance with things that previous generations would have resolved without a second thought.

Just as housework and child care continue to fall outside paid work (and are consequently devalued – although attempts are always being made to quantify the cost to families, and expanding subsidised nurseries and child-minders are seen as a way of getting parents back into work), so helping others on the basis of knowing that one day you might need help yourself meant that much of what would today be called skilled nursing and home care had passed unnoticed prior to the institutionalisation of Health. Not only did the true cost become apparent very quickly, but a service provided as of right also created expectations that could not be fulfilled.

People came to see government as being totally responsible for health and other services, and therefore nothing to do with them ("I pay my taxes"). They also became more likely to demand professional help sooner rather than later. A tendency towards dependence had replaced an acceptance that people helped each other, seeking skilled advice only as a last resort. Worse still, the flexibility offered by local action had been replaced by a range of bureaucratic welfare institutions that are very bad at responding to real need in practice, and frequently get in each other's way, creating a long-term casualty out of a hiccup in someone's ability to function.

As the cost of welfare began to escalate (the cost of the NHS in the UK doubled between 1997 and 2006 to £94 billion, a significant proportion of the increase going on pay rises[5]) and populations age, there has been a realisation that government and yet more government simply cannot deliver on its promises, and there is a renewed interest in the development of public, private and voluntary partnerships to both reduce expense and share out the responsibility. Voluntary and charitable work has continued over the past fifty years (the Home Office Citizenship Survey of 2003[6] estimated that 13.2 million people in England and Wales volunteered at least once a month) but its nature and scope have inevitably changed. It has colonised niche and specialist areas (such as the hospice movement, child abuse and research into specific disorders from cancer and heart disease to Parkinson's and cystic fibrosis) that are not adequately covered by government services. By their nature, such initiatives place an emphasis on professionalism and, although dependent on local groups, have a clear national focus, branding themselves with the skill of corporate giants.

This movement from small, local beginnings to national presence seems to be the career path of all successful voluntary groups. As a result, models of self-help and voluntary effort aimed at helping local communities to successfully take responsibility for and resolve the issues facing them are virtually non-existent. Individuals wishing to come together with others at the local level for the specific task of beginning to tackle local sustainability issues find that not only do they need to work out the issues for themselves (information is available, but generally aimed at a wider, less focused audience), they are having to break new ground in terms of the kind of voluntary association that is most likely to deliver results. Hardly promising soil within which to create a movement that will change the way we live; a hope made even more difficult by the legalistic framework that our impersonal world has made necessary.

Too Much Law, Too Little Justice

One of the prime functions (and justifications) of the state is to provide peace and security for its citizens, protecting them from external attack and from theft and violence within. To achieve that, there has to be a measure of agreement within society as to what is and isn't acceptable (and who actually "owns" certain "property"). That isn't always assured and there are likely to be clashes of interest that can, in extreme circumstances, lead to the extinction of certain ways of life. The nomad and the settler, for example, are never going to coexist peacefully and, despite long and often bloody rearguard actions, the itinerant inevitably succumbs. Likewise the value put on life and property has varied, particularly during times of civil unrest.

Nevertheless, a person's body and possessions have generally been seen as inviolable and systems evolved to provide restitution (justice) if offence to either had been caused (trial by ordeal and by combat being amongst the earliest). How seriously a claimed injury might be considered and how vigorously it was pursued would depend on who you were (your relationship with the powerful – the poor saw little in the way of redress, but then they were considered to have little to lose anyway) and how far from the seat of power you were (some areas, even in settled times, effectively ran their own systems of justice, paying little heed to central authority). England provided one of the first examples of a coherent legal and tax-gathering system – based on justices of the peace, sheriffs and local and regional assizes – to emerge from the Dark Ages in Western Europe, which is why it was such a prize to the Normans and why they were able to impose their will though relatively few in number.

Recourse to the law, however, was usually seen as the last resort, when all other options were exhausted. It could be expensive, and was generally feared and mistrusted. The portrayal of the remorseless, baffling, almost mystical workings of the Court of Chancery in Dickens's *Bleak House*[7] reflected a common view of the law as a world in itself, with the only winners being the lawyers. Except for major grievances, the law was to be steered well clear of. Most arguments were resolved unofficially using intermediaries such as the local priest, or else festered on, blighting lives, sometimes for generations.

With the advent of the first police forces in the nineteenth century, our current justice system was essentially in place. To the law, the courts in which to weight the arguments based on the law together with legal precedent, and the prisons to punish the guilty, was added an investigating arm to gather the evidence and a quasi-military organisation to ensure the accused answered the charges made against them. The system had always been hierarchical in nature (laws made centrally by government and their interpretation overseen by central appeal courts) but, with the increase in population noted in Chapter Two, combined with rising educational standards and more egalitarian social relations generally, they also became increasingly bureaucratic. As more and more justice was dispensed, so it was necessary to ensure that the basis of those judgements, the law, was seen to be interpreted uniformly across society.

Until the 1960s, going to the law remained the exception rather than the rule. People went because they had to. They were either accused of a crime or were in a dispute over property or their personal circumstances (marriage, custody of children) that they could resolve in no other way. The liberalisation that occurred across a range of issues in the 1960s – from the relaxing of censorship to the recognition of homosexuality, from easier divorce to a more child-centred view of the position of children – certainly gave rise to a less hypocritical and more tolerant society, but it also produced a shift in the position of the law. For a start more people were exposed to it (today two out of five marriages will end in divorce[8]), making it a more common, if no less pleasant, experience and, in its attempt to be responsive to real need, it became ever more nuanced and complex.

That mainstreaming of the legal process continued in the following decades until it was something that more and more people took for granted as a fact of life. As local communities continued to fragment, individuals found themselves increasingly unable to resolve their disputes with others. Not only did they no longer know, or even necessarily recognise, the individuals and groups that were causing them offence, any consensus on what constituted reasonable behaviour (the basis of resolving differences) appeared to have gone out of the window. On a whole range of issues – noise, litter, vandalism, drunkenness, abuse, foul language – it seemed as though anything went and there was nothing and no one who could do anything about it. The response to the growth of "yob culture" has been to introduce a whole raft of new legal measures to restrict antisocial behaviour.

The flip side of this criminalising of activity that could and should be resolved privately has been the growth in litigation resulting from accidents. If the law can be invoked to deal with people who are causing one physical and emotion pain, apparently intentionally, then it is a small step to using it to deal with unintended hurt – especially when there is money involved. From there it no distance at all to assuming that someone else is to blame for all one's difficulties and that it is the responsibility of the courts to make it all better. Taken to its extreme it offers an inhuman picture of people prepared to go to law at any perceived hurt or provocation. In some people's minds we're already there.

The law is expanding in other ways. As organisations of all kinds have grown bigger, so has the necessity to police them. Coupled with a recognition that the impact that polluters make, for example, can be far reaching, this increasing will to impose centrally determined standards and interfere with the day-to-day workings of all activities outside the home (although these are included as soon as we employ someone to decorate our house or do even elementary repairs) has resulted in yet more legislation and a myriad of agencies that can take individuals and companies to court. More recently, the threat of terrorism has added yet more layers of regulation, ranging from mere nuisance value (slowing down the time it takes to open a bank account) to downright infringement of civil liberties (the ability to hold someone indefinitely without charge).

It wouldn't matter so much if going to court actually resolved problems. One of the myths about the legal system is that it is an effective way of finding the truth. It isn't. What it does do very well is to look at a situation from its own narrow perspective, redefine it according to what it sees to be important and then ask the question "has something happened?" If it has then the law will act although, even then, its focus may not reflect the priorities of the party that has brought the grievance. The strength of the case is then tested in an adversarial encounter, in which the legal experts representing both parties will have an interest in casting doubt on their opponent's veracity and in using the theatre of the court to generate sympathy for their point of view. It may lack the drama of a televised courtroom series but it is just as unreal, especially when you consider that many cases are decided on technicalities rather than issues. It is, in fact, a closed system.

Given the chance, real people try to sort out their differences by trying to understand the other's point of view, rather than destroy it. There is a natural tendency to try to find common ground rather than polarising opinions even further. And there is usually a willingness to make concessions for the sake of reaching an understanding; a position that is far removed from the win or lose of the courtroom. It is hardly surprising that, even when people win their case, they are left feeling dissatisfied, as if their point of view hasn't really been listened to and there has been no true resolution of the grievance. The feelings of the losers can be a smouldering animosity that informs their dealings with others for some time to come.

On the one hand, our legal system is beginning to collapse under the weight of legislation; on the other, individuals no longer seem to be able to resolve the simplest of problems without recourse to the law. It isn't a healthy situation and it has come about because we no longer have a vibrant and viable civil society to mediate between people and find common-sense solutions to their problems. Once a community loses the ability to keep watch over itself, to informally identify and deal with aberrant behaviour, it has given up its autonomy and it inevitably becomes prey to the arbitrary workings of the powerful, whether they be the courts and the police, or supermarkets, or the ever expanding army of officials charged with monitoring every aspect of public life. For all our so-called individual freedoms we can, at any hour and any minute, fall into the hands of others who are unlikely to be sympathetic to who we are and what we consider to be important. We have become powerless.

From the foregoing it is clear that civil society, the only medium through which we, as individuals, might yet reverse the headlong rush towards catastrophe, has been squeezed to the margins and is generally in a pretty bad shape. But it is not yet dead and, while there is life, there is hope. Beneath the life-threatening, almost random actions of the global economy and the imperial aspirations of the political system, real people are doing what they've always done; getting on with life and making the best of a bad job. To do that they instinctively try to connect with others and, however poor the soil, seek to ameliorate their lot through association. That is and always has been a source of potential energy. To return to the social magnet analogy, the task is to coax that energy into alignment so that it might be turned to a useful purpose, namely creating the kind of secure, sustainable lifestyles that we all intuitively recognise is what we want.

That will require change and plenty of it. From the analysis to date it should be clear that our existing forms of governance just aren't capable of delivering it. They are on autopilot – many closed systems contributing to one huge one, rushing along regardless of the consequences.

So how can we go about halting the runaway train? To answer that question we must first consider how change takes place and how best it can be nurtured.

5

The Seeds of Change

We have freedom of choice, so it is claimed, and yet our decision-making processes, as exemplified by our economic, political and social systems, appear to be pushing us remorselessly in a single direction and one that is ultimately unsustainable. Common sense suggests that we must change course. But is there an alternative, and can we really stand out against the tide? How can we, as individuals, make a difference when the forces ranged against us are so powerful? Can we, in fact, change anything?

One way of looking at these questions is to recognise that change is a condition of existence. Even in the most static and stable of times there is an ongoing battle between order and chaos; people have to continually build and repair just to keep on top of the natural processes of waste and decay. Our own era, by comparison, is one of unremitting change. One only has to look back over the past two hundred years to see the distance that has been covered in Western society. Someone living in 1800 would have been born into a largely agrarian society in which the main source of motive power remained the animal; they would have been influenced by the ideas coming out of the American and

French Revolutions, while being under no illusion that power still lay with land, wealth and breeding, whichever continent they were on; the nearest town would have been their only trading point, life would have revolved around craft work and self-sufficiency, and mutual aid was all that people had to fall back on when times were hard.

A hundred years later, in 1900, a majority of the population lived in towns and cities (in itself an indication of a striking shift in the way people thought and acted), time was determined by the clock rather than the sun, and the factory system was the dominant form of organisation. International trade and competition were linked to expanding empires and money was being invested around the world. Mass-produced, manufactured goods were replacing hand-crafted wares. Although most women in the USA and Great Britain would have to wait until after the First World War to vote, universal suffrage was now an established principle. Power lay with a new class of paternalistic entrepreneur, prominent individuals and families who owned vast enterprises and determined the lives of thousands of workers – offset to some extent by the rise in trade unionism. Society was becoming more complex, but the broad outlines of decision-making remained well defined. Many didn't like the way things were moving, others felt that they were happening too slowly, but there was nevertheless a general perception that a better world could be created. Progress was something worth pursuing.

At the beginning of the twenty-first century, it is easy to see that there has been further, rapid change. However, any confidence that may have existed about our continuing ability to improve the human lot has long since evaporated in the face of endless images of war and genocide, and our seemingly limitless capacity for cruelty and barbarism. Beneath our confident exterior the times are altogether less certain and fear of strangers is apparent everywhere. Technology nevertheless dominates our lives, and most people in the West lead lifestyles that would have been unimaginable to their forebears. Money has become the universal medium of exchange and individualism has triumphed, expressing itself through the consumption of an ever-expanding array of mass-produced, material goods. Power has shifted to the corporate world, faceless people whose sources of influence are obscure, and who keep away from the public gaze. Rafts of legislation to "protect" the public from the worst excesses of this depersonalised world – health and safety, political correctness, environmental health, building control, etc. – spawn bureaucratic monoliths that trample across ordinary lives in their zeal to perform their limited and limiting functions.

Yet, for all this evidence of remarkable change, it is arguable that it is nothing more than the ongoing emergence and development of themes that were already well established by 1800. An eight-hundred and fifty-seater Airbus A380, capable of spanning continents, is only a development of the frail biplane that first carried the Wright brothers into the air – which, in turn, was only made possible by a scientific mindset that placed careful observation and experiment above faith and superstition. Once set in train, such movements take on a life and logic of their own that can, in themselves, become closed systems, creating the conditions in which the people in their thrall are unable or unwilling to see the dangers that their continuing enthusiasm for a particular way of thinking and acting is creating. We have inherited a world view that has produced a technology capable of bringing unprecedented material benefits to some, but which chooses to routinely use the same skills, not only to oppress, maim and kill our fellow human beings in unprecedented numbers, but to rape and destroy the planet that is the only hope of life for our children and grandchildren.

Current systems of decision-making are the product of a mindset that has been evolving in the West from the Renaissance onwards. There is little evidence that they are capable of rising to the challenges that they themselves have created. It follows that the task is to fundamentally change the way we think and act, not merely to change the emphasis of the existing ways in which we all habitually respond to the world around us. Rather than add further detail to the already complex picture our civilisation has painted, particularly over the past two hundred years, we need the vision with which to begin a new one altogether. It's a tall order and such transformations only happen infrequently in human history.

So where do we begin? With ourselves is the simple answer, and particularly with how it is that we come to see the world in certain ways, how that affects the way we act, and how we might change those mind maps. Understanding these fundamental aspects of our functioning as human beings will hopefully suggest some ways in which we might do things differently.

All in the Mind?

We are embodied creatures, made of flesh and blood, and that both defines and limits our potential. One only has to look at the impact of hormones on a group of male deer at the beginning of the rutting season – turning them from sociable companions to deadly rivals – to understand something of the implications of that statement. We are also, as far as we know, alone in Nature in possessing consciousness to a degree that has allowed us to step outside and largely ignore our animal heritage.

But what does it mean to be conscious? During the Enlightenment of the eighteenth century, consciousness came to be seen as the seat of reason and, as such, the hope for humankind. To apply reason to our situation would surely create heaven on Earth. A careful, conscious study of reality, free from blind faith, superstition and prejudice, became what we call the scientific project. That approach, as we have seen, changed the way we live. Not only has it given humans an undreamt-of mastery over their environment – wiping out killer diseases and speeding up communications to the point where we can see what is happening on the other side of the globe as it takes place (in 1805, it took more than nine days for news of the victory at Trafalgar to reach the Admiralty, and two weeks for it to appear in the newspapers), it has also created a materialistic way of looking at the world that has brought us to the brink of disaster. That slow, dawning realisation is having its effect. Although we continue to preach rationality as the only basis for human action, as a culture we no longer truly believe our own message: we have lost faith with reason.

Who we perceive ourselves to be depends on our beliefs and, in the final analysis, people are prepared to die rather than admit they're wrong. So different ways of looking at the world have to be acknowledged and taken seriously, even when we don't share them. But where do they come from? That, of course, depends on your beliefs about the nature of being human! In other words, we have to begin with assumptions that other people can then accept or reject. The following statements are intended to provide such a starting point. They have been chosen as examples of areas where there are opposing and equally strongly held points of view and where one's stance will profoundly affect any strategy for change:

a) Human nature seeks life (but that doesn't mean we aren't capable of dealing out death and destruction, both as individuals and societies!)

To state that the life force is ultimately creative and that we are part of that grand design is ultimately a matter of faith. But, as Gandhi (1869-1948) suggested, "it is the law of love that rules humankind. Had violence, i.e. hatred ruled us, we should have become extinct long ago."[1] But we have to work at it.

A belief that, even at the eleventh hour, it is possible to find a way for us all to live securely and harmoniously on this crowded planet thus implies having a basic faith in Life and humanity's place in it. There are plenty of views about our current predicament that suggest it is pointless to do anything. James Lovelock, author of Gaia and champion of the Earth as a self-regulating organism, has stated that it is already too late to counter the worst effects of climate change. Others see humans as incapable of acting selflessly and predict that, when the situation begins to deteriorate, it will be everyone for themselves and the weak will go to the wall. Some evangelical Christians go so far as to see evidence of the Second Coming in the increasing incidence of war, environmental collapse and climate change and hold their hands out in welcome, believing that their God will intervene to spare his creatures suffering before things get too bad. A common theme is that civilisation as we know it will be wiped away. And not before time for those who see us as decadent, weak and morally bankrupt.

We are never going to create a heaven on earth – we are far too flawed for that – but a belief that human nature is basically life affirming is fundamental to the desire to want to live differently and in a way that minimises the dangers we currently face. All too soon we will become complacent once again and fall into the habitual ways of responding to life's difficulties that will inevitably contain the seeds of yet further challenges down the line. But life will go on and our children will live in circumstances that we would recognise as having value.

b) We are more than the sum of our genes (but our genetic makeup is important!)

Whether we are the product of nature or nurture remains an open question. For the moment, the view that we are simply the product of our genes (i.e. nature) is in the ascendant with the implication that, if only we knew enough about an individual's genetic makeup, we could predict their behaviour in any given set of circumstances. In practice, that tells us very little, because the number of variables that would have to be taken into account is just too large to handle.

To understand something of the complexity of the debate, let us assume for a moment that life is like a game of cards in which we are each dealt a genetic hand and we have to play our cards as best we can. How we do that will depend on the game currently in town (i.e. the culture we are part of and which values some cards higher than others), our understanding of the rules and our ability to use them to our own advantage (our social position, our education in the widest sense and our self-confidence) and the cards that others at the table have to play. Starting off with a simple idea – cards as genes – we have quickly built up a many-layered metaphor that embraces both what is happening within us and outside in the wider world, our own personal history as well as that of the society we inhabit, and the nature of the immediate relationships around us. We are held in a complicated web of potential outcomes and, as in a real game of cards, the result is never assured, even when we believe we are holding a winning hand.

This statement is important because it challenges a growing assumption that our behaviours are in some ways wholly determined by our genes – that we may have no choice but to commit anti-social acts such as murder. Such a viewpoint denies the existence of a moral universe (see pages 106-109).

c) Most of human activity is unconscious (but that doesn't mean we act irrationally!)

We need to acknowledge that consciousness (in the sense of having perception and being aware) doesn't play the central role that some observers have ascribed to it. That is why hopes for a better future based on reason alone are likely to be overly optimistic.

There is evidence, for example, that we become aware of what we are about to say a few milliseconds *after* the muscles necessary for speech have been activated. That doesn't imply that we routinely engage our mouths before our brains, but it does suggest that consciousness isn't necessarily at the forefront of the process. When we learn to speak or read a foreign language, the process is slow and evidently self-conscious. We are literally selecting the words one by one and then assembling them in what we believe to be the correct order. Eventually, however, our speech starts to flow and become spontaneous; we have internalised the new language and become sufficiently proficient that we only become aware of what we are doing when we stumble over a word or phrase.

Looking at how we behave (i.e. reviewing our actions consciously) may help us to understand ourselves and thereby choose to try and do things differently (to change the way we do things), but it is impossible to live that way on a minute-by-minute basis. Particularly in our relationships, we deploy a range of largely unconscious responses – empathy, intuition, etc. In practice, we act in a holistic fashion, responding to the complexities of existence from our whole beings. Our consciousness is part of that process and, in certain limited circumstances, it may be helpful to rely solely on that capacity to detach ourselves. As a general way of relating to the world around us, however, it is likely to be less helpful, and much of the argument thus far suggests that our present state of affairs is the direct result of our having relied on the so-called light of reason too much. That is not to say that we should abandon scepticism for credulity, or stop trying to think through what we are trying to do. Rather it is saying that what happens in the real world is vastly more complicated and fast moving than we assume and trying to consciously work out what is going on can be a bit like comparing the dietary benefits of the various foods available to us in the middle of a hurricane.

Moving Swiftly On

Having acknowledged that what we believe about human nature will influence how we set about the task of trying to live more sustainably, we are now in a position to explore why it is that we find change, any change, so difficult. As a starting point, we need to recognise that we are creatures of habit. We routinely approach the world on the basis of assumptions, both about what our senses tell us is out there (this object is a chair) and the meanings we attach to our perceptions (it is something to sit on). In that sense we operate as if everything were *un*changing and, in reality, we don't have time to check out everything we come across (by and large, things that look like chairs turn out to be chairs). The same is true of less tangible assumptions about the world (it is a safe or dangerous place to be); a person who approaches life in a trusting way will generally have that view reinforced by experience, but so will someone who assumes that there are hazards around every corner. We also tend to have fixed and unchanging views about the world we inhabit (politics, religion, cultural preferences) that reflect and reinforce the ways we habitually respond to the situations we face.

Making assumptions about objects like chairs is relatively straightforward; we have grown up with them – they are literally part of our mental furniture. How we come to have a general orientation towards life (based on trust or fear, for example) can equally be understood in terms of our upbringing and experiences at key times in our lives. But how do more concrete beliefs such as political and religious certainties and attitudes towards abortion, immigration and murder come into being?

There's little new in life, and a moment's thought suggests that all the issues we are ever likely to face have been fought over and debated in one guise or another throughout the ages. Thinkers have created frameworks within which to explain and analyse them, and simplified versions of these have passed into the vernacular ("it's the rich what gets the pleasure, it's the poor what gets the blame"). People at different times have followed what they understood to be the precepts of the Utilitarians, the Marxists and the Existentialists, for example, and each in turn has been supplanted by another credo. The fact that no one has come up with a wholly adequate formula for dealing with life's problems suggests that there probably isn't one that holds good for all occasions and all times – but that won't stop people from trying!

Whether we choose one set of beliefs or another depends on what options are available to us at the time and who we are as people. If there is a choice (communism vs. capitalism, for example) we will probably feel instinctively more comfortable with one perspective than the other and that has to do with the environment of ideas and images that we have grown up with. As we reach adulthood we begin to experience ourselves as autonomous beings, able to strike out on our own. The world is full of possibilities, or so it seems. But we embark on that journey with a weight of history that we are largely unconscious of.

As we grow and develop, we uncritically absorb much of what happens around us, gaining cues from our immediate care givers about how they feel about life (whether they are generally happy, afraid, optimistic, etc.) and gaining a sense of what they approve of and what they don't (without necessarily understanding the reasons why). Our outlook on life is being subtly but firmly channelled. In a family where these distinctions are clear cut, for example, the child is more likely to become rigid in their thinking, seeing issues in black and white and being dogmatic in their beliefs.

As well as absorbing the emotional climate around us, we must also accommodate the attitudes, prejudices and views of the wider social milieu we inhabit (which might be at odds with those of our parents), and such accumulated family and cultural history as has significance for us. All that baggage is far from neutral. If our experiences and the messages we have received during our childhood have been negative, we are more likely to reach adulthood with a poor self-image, low self-esteem and a consequent lack of confidence. Often issues run in families, passing problems from generation to generation.

What we internalise in this way can then affect our ability to solve the problems we face, and the views that we have inherited from our collective past can limit the kind of responses that are open to us. The social arrangements of which we are a part, including the institutions that society has evolved, may also restrict the options available. All these limitations are rarely available at the conscious level and it comes as no surprise, therefore, that we find it hard to change the way we act, even in the face of threat. We have become fixed in a particular posture towards the world and we look to those around us, the social structures of which we are a part and our wider culture to reflect and reinforce it, rejecting anyone or any social construct (e.g. political party) that fails to do that (that is one reason why particular peoples are said to have national or racial characteristics).

In practice, our everyday lives are prescribed by the following four dimensions of perception. While they limit the way we look at the world, they also hint at how change can take place: alter one aspect and it has an impact on the others. From small beginnings significant change can occur.

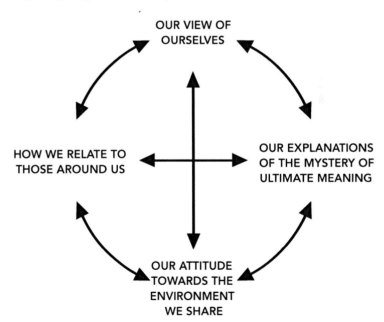

Despite the superficial flurry of change that is all about us, it is clear that our basic orientation as a culture is fixed and unyielding, and has been for some time now. We view ourselves, first and foremost, as individualised with certain entitlements and rights. That leads us to see others as separate from us, part of informal networks of association which place few obligations upon us. The environment is there for our benefit and to provide us with the means to enjoy the good life, while our explanations of life are largely materialistic, emphasising the importance of detachment from our surroundings whether they be other humans, animals or nature itself.

In the Eye of the Beholder

So how do we go about changing? One way of exploring that question is to invoke the Gestalt image of lines on a piece of paper that appear to depict an ugly crone. Look at it again and you see a beautiful woman. You may need it pointing out to you but, once you've seen it, a genuine shift in your perception has taken place and you will always be able to see the beautiful woman if you so choose. The lines on the page – reality – remain the same, what we see has radically altered. That is what a change in world-view means. It is a Divine Right of Kings Moment and our perspective has altered. As a consequence, what we consider important will be different too. And as we begin to behave differently in response to these changed priorities, so new possibilities open up (our attitude to those around may be subtly altered, as may our perception of the environment around us and the way we explain what it means to be alive – and each of these changes in turn will influence how we view ourselves) and, providing we keep true to our vision, an ever-expanding range of challenges and opportunities will require us to change even more. It can happen without us being conscious of the distance we have travelled.

Just as the beautiful woman was there all along – we just didn't see her – we aren't being asked to invent something that doesn't exist. We are being asked to see what currently we can't – and then to have the courage to act on what we perceive. Cromwell (1599-1658) and the other Puritans finally, and only after much heart-searching, concluded that the only way to deal with a King they believed to have blood on his hands was to remove him. On that cold, winter's day in 1649, on a scaffold erected outside the Banqueting Hall in Whitehall, human history changed irrevocably. Monarchy may have been restored to Britain only nine years later, but the introduction of a *constitutional* monarchy with the Glorious Revolution of 1688 would hardly have been possible without that dramatic act. And the American and French Revolutions may not have occurred when and in the way they did without it – a fundamental shift in thinking had occurred. Whatever the merits or demerits of kingship, it wasn't a divinely ordained state of affairs. It therefore followed that kings (and other rulers for that matter) had to be limited and regulated by human perceptions of what was just and reasonable.

So what are we being asked to see? At present we inhabit a world dominated by the big battalions, espousing consciousness, order, predictability and detachment – all the virtues of the scientific mindset applied quite inappropriately to wider reality – in which human beings no longer count. It is selfish, individualistic and competitive: an ugly old crone indeed, albeit one dressed with all the glitter and allure that the material world can offer. But enfolded within the relentless, frenetic activity and the boundless energy in pursuit of the novel, other images can be glimpsed; ones that speak of closeness, involvement, engagement and individual creativity, all the things, in fact, that we associate with being human and which have never entirely deserted us. We continue to feel those needs. Now is the time to make them central to the way our societies are structured.

Our everyday speech is something we can consciously change and, though apparently unnatural at first, we not only come to use these news words and phrases with ease, but we internalise some of the reasoning behind the changes (as with learning a foreign language mentioned above). There are several themes that, taken together, offer an insight into the kind of shift in thinking that will be necessary if the destructive forces currently in play are to be reversed. We need to begin to grapple with the implications of the following –

a) Recognising that large is likely to be dangerous:

Over two thousand three hundred years ago, Aristotle (384-322 BCE) wrote in his Politics "To the size of states there is a limit, as there is to other things, plants, animals, implements; for none of these retain their natural power when they are too large or too small, but they either wholly lose their nature, or are spoiled."[2] Entranced by the giddy sense of power that technology has placed in our hands, we have lost that sense of appropriate scale and are reaping the consequences. We automatically accept that big is best because everywhere we look we are dwarfed by our own structures, whether physical, social or moral.

Beyond a certain point, Nature evolves not by getting bigger, but by getting more complex. In all natural systems there a limit to growth that, once exceeded, actually restricts complexity. That tendency is evident everywhere in our economic, political and social structures that have long since passed the point where they can become more complex, attempting instead to cope with their mounting inefficiency with ever more central control.

Increasing size in Nature is functional only in so far as it enhances survival. Once that point has been passed natural processes automatically bring the situation back into balance. Our systems do not conform to that basic rule; they keep on getting bigger, which is a sure sign that we have passed beyond what is natural and occupy an increasingly unreal world that is detached from life itself.

b) Changing the emphasis from mechanistic to organic images:

Traditional science underpins our technological society. Without it the glittering array of electronic gadgetry, stylish cars, jumbo jets and vast civil engineering projects across the globe would be simply impossible. A long time ago, in the Victorian era, you could see the application of science with your own eyes and understand the principles that guided the technology. Today, style seeks to hide or soften the function of a piece of machinery and, in the process, reveals nothing about how it works.

Technology has moved beyond the ability of the average person in the street (few people now repair their own cars or domestic machinery), and the insights that are coming back from the frontiers of theoretical science suggest a strange, unpredictable universe of extra dimensions and singularities quite unlike the traditional structures built on endlessly replicable proofs. Yet our culture continues to think in the old, Victorian ways of taking things apart and putting them back together. Mechanistic images reveal that legacy; we speak of things going "as smooth as clockwork", of "steaming ahead" and "don't fix it if it isn't broken". Such figures of speech are symptomatic of a way of thinking that is:-

- inherently hierarchical and organised top-down (some parts are more important than others and they determine the nature of the enterprise; there is a need to organise the parts into a whole and continually monitor their performance)

- interventionist (if a part is perceived to have problems it is the role of the more important parts to sort them out)

- reductionist (the whole is only the sum of its parts),

- simplistic (if we understand the parts we will understand the whole),

- functionalist (each part is separate and has its own distinct function), and

- linear (systems are consciously organised in such a way that a follows from b and leads to c and, as a consequence, are quite impervious to what is happening elsewhere in the world).

It is easy to see the ways in which our bureaucratic monoliths and their decision-making processes revolve around these assumptions about the nature of existence, which is one reason why they continually seek uniformity, conformity and stability when the world plainly isn't like that. It also explains why they find difficulty in adapting to changed circumstances.

By contrast, an organic perspective puts the emphasis on:-

- self-regulation (each part is capable of organising itself and fitting in harmoniously with the other parts)

- the ability to self-repair (each part has the potential within itself to look after itself)

- interdependence (each part is interconnected with and has an influence on every other part)

- the whole being made up of its parts, each of which may consist of a number of smaller parts, each of which is also quite properly self-regulating, self-repairing and interdependent

- the whole being greater than and different from the sum of the parts

- the well-being of the whole being dependent on the well-being of each of the parts – in that sense, one part cannot be said to be superior to, or in control of the others

- circularity (it is a learning entity, continually changing in response to feedback both internally and externally), and as a consequence

- adaptability being built into the organism

Thus, an organism isn't a random set of events, it is balancing act between the autonomy of the parts and the needs of the whole (the parts, after all, are meaningless without the existence of the whole). Individual organisms may not always achieve that balance perfectly (most individuals are born with disabilities of one sort or another), but the species as a whole is capable of getting the balance right and is continually seeking to adapt in the face of a changing environment. Organic decision-making systems that seek to achieve that balance are always more likely to be successful (especially when dealing with change) than mechanistic ones that are dominated by a relentlessly vigilant centre.

c) Accepting that we occupy a bi-polar world and that reality is a balancing act between opposites

Each and every day is a struggle. We instinctively recognise and accept that insight both as individuals and organisations. What we don't usually realise – because we operate within a traditional scientific mindset that emphasises order and certainty – is that the difficulties that we continually face are, at root, the inevitable consequence of living in a world of polar opposites (self/other, good/evil, life/death, suspicion/trust, etc.). Everywhere we look there are opposites and it isn't simply a question of deciding which pole to choose – to be "good", for example – because each defines and is defined by the other. Both "good" and "evil" exist in the world in the sense that we embody within us the potential for both (Nazi Germany is an example of how "evil" can come to dominate an entire society). However, to try and be "good" at all costs risks doing "evil" without even being aware of it. It can, for example, lead to the kind of rigidity in outlook that shuns anything that is seen as "evil" and, in the process, turns its back on some of the qualities that are usually associated with "goodness" – charity, tolerance and sympathy.

It's hard enough to try to reach one pole along a single dimension such as "goodness" and "evil". It becomes impossible and pointless when we see that we are surrounded by an almost infinite number of such dimensions, each demanding that we make choices that will impact on the others. The more extreme a position we take on any one dimension, the more likely we are to create problems both for ourselves and those around us. That isn't to say that we should just give up and go with the flow. In that direction lies an inevitable slide into the destructive aspects of reality – chaos, selfishness, paranoia, etc. Life is a constant battle between the forces of life and death, with the latter the winner by default if we don't stand up firmly and steadfastly for the former. But death is part of life and, if we try and deny that fact, we run the danger of unconsciously creating a death-like state of existence – which is one way of describing the way we are heading today.

The bi-polar nature of reality presents us with a constant challenge, and the choices we make are important. Just as the myriad decisions that each of us takes every day about how to spend our money sends messages that influence the whole money economy, so the life choices we take directly contribute to how life-affirming our social fabric is. In the struggle that is life, an ability to navigate and balance the ever-shifting matrix of forces that we experience might be one definition of success.

In the following areas our society is potentially seriously *imbalanced*:-

- Order versus Chaos

If life is a balancing act it is, by definition, a hazardous enterprise; there is always the possibility of getting it wrong and falling to one side or the other. To achieve the balance between the autonomy of the parts and the needs of the whole, we risk sliding into either chaos or order. If the parts have too much autonomy, the integrity of the organism will disappear and it will die; if they have too little autonomy, control will assert itself and bring stagnation in its wake, leaving the organism vulnerable to the challenge of external threat or change. Fortunately the margin for error is usually sufficient for sensitive feedback systems to sound the alarm in time for remedial action to be taken. Success, however, is not assured and real-life organisms die because they prove to be insufficiently adaptable. The price of trying to negotiate a path between chaos and order is eternal vigilance.

The arthritic nature of our institutions suggests that we have currently got the balance wrong.

- Cooperation versus Competition

That the global economy is predicated solely on competition is obvious from the effects that modern living has on our social and environmental fabric. To pursue the dream of consumerist heaven requires, so the argument runs, the lubricant of competitiveness to keep producers mean and lean. Only in that way can costs be kept down, the endlessly changing vistas of fashion-driven consumption sustained and the borrowing needed to keep the whole show on the road stimulated. But it is far from the open competition that the free marketeers advocate. For a start, the big corporations seek to control the market through a combination of sheer size and muscle and the legal and economic framework in which the game is played. That means that some players end up with tremendous power and can effectively dictate terms to the others who seek only to survive at the margins.

The same is true at the individual level where a few (us) are doing very nicely, thank you at the expense of the many (them). Because competition fosters greed and a need for endless material accumulation, those of us in the driving seat have very little incentive to change direction. Even if we did recognise a sense of fellow feeling with them, we have lost the means to do anything about it. We deal with the essentially competitive nature of our society, not by looking for opportunities to cooperate, but by burying ourselves in routines, dreaming of careers and promotion paths and getting away from it all.

Competition is inherent to life, but there are healthy and unhealthy varieties. We pride ourselves on being part of successful organisations that span the country if not the world, but fail to see that they lack a human core; they do not exist to meet the human need for association and collaborative effort, but follow a logic that is devoid of any characteristics that we might call human – in the final analysis they are anti-life.

We are simply in denial about the damage we are doing to ourselves, those around us and the environment we share, and have lost the ability to act cooperatively to do something about it.

• Engagement versus Detachment

We have created a mindset that allows us to use technology to exploit our fellow humans and destroy our environment. That detachment from the consequences of our actions hasn't happened by accident, but is the direct consequence of two inter-related and long-term trends in Western society – the move to cities and the gradual dominance of what might be called a traditional scientific-materialist mindset. Urbanisation doesn't in itself cut people off from Nature – the countryside was after all an ever-present, noisy and messy presence in medieval cities – but patterns of living that have completely severed that direct link with a surrounding hinterland inevitably lead to a perception of the natural world as external and other (as an example of how divorced we have become from nature, research has shown that schoolchildren can identify common birds only if they feature regularly on television or logos). When any sense of communal responsibility, even for the street we live in, is removed by the provision of public services, our detachment from our environment is complete (we live in a sort of bubble that insulates us from the external world).

Everyday life, by its nature, requires a degree of detachment. We have to stand back in order to make judgements, but there is always a balance between that and engaging fully with those around us. By comparison, the way the scientific method has developed has put an absolute premium on detachment, even in the study of ourselves and other living creatures, and that emphasis has come to dominate everyday life. That has had all kinds of implications for what we consider important and leads directly to the kind of thinking that produces the problems now apparent in the economic, political and social spheres.

The task is to find a way of looking at the world that allows us to use technology to coexist in peace, security and harmony with others and the environment on which we all depend.

• Masculine principle versus Feminine principle

Taking an overview of the imbalances that exist in our world, it is hard to escape the conclusion that the biggest imbalance of all is the bias towards the masculine principle. Rationality, order, competition, law, detachment and hierarchy all dominate, while it is increasingly difficult to see evidence of the feminine principle (engagement, mystery, nurturing, co-operation and reciprocity) anywhere on our social landscape.

The two principles aren't directly related to gender, but the fact that women (who would generally be expected to be more sympathetic to the feminine virtues) are being successfully absorbed into this essentially masculine way of thinking and acting merely dilutes the feminine energy available generally. It is ironic that we appear to have moved from patriarchy (in which men dominated women) to a social order governed by the masculine principle (whether it's men or women controlling it). Just as the global economy is empire masquerading as equity, so democracy (which should be about balance) is really the masculine principle under another name. It is time we genuinely sought a balance between the two principles.

d) Understanding that there is strength in diversity

To cope with the inherent messiness of life our society has sought to achieve order through uniformity. That hasn't necessarily been a conscious process, there are plenty of processes pushing us in that direction – from centralised law-making delivered through an ever widening net of regulation that has to be policed, to the globalisation of the economy itself and the stranglehold that a few large corporations exert over everything from what is shown in our cinemas to the increasingly undifferentiated look of our town centres, from the homogenising effects of international travel to the monoculture nature of agri-business. It is also true in our personal associations that are dominated by employment, where similar work practices, knowledge and expertise, shaped by corporate emphasis tend to produce groups with essentially similar outlooks.

Such arrangements are inherently vulnerable to change. The greater the diversity in a natural system the more likely it is to be able to influence and restrict the factors that might lead to change in the first place. The Earth itself can be seen as one vast regulatory organism that has successfully maintained the conditions for life over the millennia. Only our inability to do the same has produced the circumstances where even a system so robust might be overwhelmed.

In every aspect of human life, from our personal relationships to our communities, from our overarching economic and political systems to our cultural imperatives, we need to reassess how we encourage true diversity as a matter of urgency.

Going for Change

Very impressionistically, we have seen some of the dimensions we will have to explore if we are to rebalance our approach to the world and create a more life enhancing mindset.

a) recognising that large is likely to be dangerous

b) changing the emphasis from mechanistic to organic images

c) accepting that we occupy a bi-polar world and that reality is a balancing act between opposites, and

d) understanding that there is strength in diversity.

Having looked at how we come to hold particular views about the world we live in – views that we tend to get stuck with even when they are causing us harm – we can now begin to form an agenda for change by asking three simple questions:-

e) WHAT are we trying to achieve?

f) WHY are we trying to achieve it?

g) HOW, in the light of the answers to the first two questions, should we set about achieving it?

Many individuals and groups go straight to the last question because they assume they know the answer to the first two. And confusion inevitably results because participants in the process inevitably come with different perceptions, priorities, timetables and interests. Unless a common view of what is important can be established at the outset, one that everyone can sign up to and support, the outcome will be an inevitable fudging of the issues and the creation of further, avoidable problems down the line. The clearer the answers to the first two questions (and the greater the honesty exhibited in reaching them), the more likely it is that sensible answers to the third will emerge – and that takes time.

So WHAT are we trying to achieve – what will be a positive outcome? If we go back to Chapter 1, the answer to that question is that we are seeking to successfully rise to the various challenges that currently face us. That, in turn, means finding a way to learn to live sustainably – defined as:-

the maintenance of a quality life both now and into the future

maintaining that quality life in a just and equitable manner across the globe

maintaining that quality life within the capacities of local, regional and global ecosystems, and

taking the long term view.

From an individual perspective – and we are trying to provide an answer to the question "what can we, as individuals, do?" – a simple way of framing the WHAT question would thus be to say "we want everyone to be able to live securely and sustainably on this crowded planet" (with the definition of sustainability given above).

It has been suggested that the reason that we are making so little impact in achieving this goal is because our governance (decision-making systems at all levels) is simply not capable of responding; it is as if it were set on autopilot and is taking us at an ever increasing speed towards disaster. The kind of governance systems that we need to adopt if we are to change that situation is part of the WHY question because the answer could lie anywhere along the spectrum of centralised, world government to complete anarchy – where we choose to place our emphasis will depend on our beliefs about the best way to solve the problem and that will come from examining what we consider to be important; in other words, our core values.

We need now to explore WHY we are seeking to achieve sustainability. What values will underpin and define our activities, and enable us to act coherently and in consort with others? That is the subject of the next chapter.

6

The WHY Question and the Human Scale

Even amongst those who recognise that the way that humankind is heading is unsustainable and leading us inevitably towards catastrophe, there is little agreement about an alternative. There are those who passionately believe that only some form of world government can halt the slide while, at the other end of the spectrum, are those who look, with equal conviction, towards a deep shift in human consciousness as our only hope of salvation.

The advantage of having a coherent world view is that it focuses the mind on a particular set of options that, by definition, exclude all others. That is its particular strength, but also its weakness. Having said, in effect, that this is the spot on which I choose to pitch my tent, I have no choice but to get on with making the best of it. By concentrating on what is immediately around me, rather than constantly gazing at far horizons, I am also more likely to bring my full energies to bear on the problems that life inevitably throws up. Of course, I could be wrong and my decision to stop here rather than somewhere else could be disastrous for both myself and others. But, ultimately, I have to make that commitment if I am to avoid lumbering around in a fog of half-glimpsed possibilities.

By taking a particular stance we are ascribing value to certain aspects of reality and diminishing the importance of others. It is important to recognise that we are doing this because it will influence the decisions we take. As we have seen, any aspect of governance can slip all too easily into becoming a closed system and it is important to have quick and effective feedback loops to ensure that we can retain the big picture and adjust what we are doing accordingly. For that reason, it is better to have an overall sense of direction than a detailed route map. If we are passing through unfamiliar territory we will need a compass bearing or an obvious landmark to aim for, but we should also be able to change our plans to be able to cope with changing circumstances; the road ahead may be flooded, or we may wish to make a diversion to something interesting we have glimpsed along the way.

We need a framework that is flexible and open-ended rather than dogmatic or prescriptive. We need an aide-mémoire – a readily accessible vision of the future we are seeking to reach – that will provide a sense of direction in the here and now, and enable us to ask the question "are we getting closer to where we want to be, or not?"

The argument developed thus far has suggested some themes around which a new world view might cohere:-

- Large is likely to be dangerous.

- We should be using an organic frame of reference rather than a mechanistic one.

- We inhabit a bi-polar world of opposites, and

- There is strength in diversity.

The broader the stretch of our connections – the greater the number of people and things we have to consider in making decisions – the more likely it is that we shall have to resort to mechanistic forms of organisation, which both simplify and dehumanise our responses to life. In other words, some form of worldwide structure based on existing models of government is, by its nature, unlikely to have the flexibility to cope with the complexity of life as it actually is. By the same token, a deeper spiritual awareness of the nature of that reality may help us appreciate what we are going to lose if we don't act, but it is unlikely to provide the language by which that insight can be translated into practice. That will happen through small, relatively stable groups of people who are committed to an ever deeper exploration of themselves, their interactions with each other and with the environment they share in common (see diagram on page 81) – and who have the opportunity to do it. It is about real people and the nature of their relationships. We are talking about something that is essentially human in scale.

Yes, we are part of a global community and we need to take account of that. The Human Scale approach suggests, however, that the best chance of achieving this goal is to concentrate on the *local* not the global, focusing on how communities at the local level can live securely and sustainably with one another, and then to apply those principles to the bigger picture, not vice versa.

The same is true of a shift in human consciousness. That has to happen, but implicit in the Human Scale approach is the belief that it is more likely to take place as part of an overall reassessment of the nature of the relationships between people at the local level and, by implication, their connection with the environment around them. Self-development and increasing awareness will come as an inevitable part of that process rather than from being an end in itself. Spirituality – the sense of awe and wonder that should underpin our basic orientation to the world we inhabit – will also assume a new significance as communities explore together the numinous that only becomes apparent once you admit to yourself that you don't know everything.

The Human Scale, then, is a term for a general orientation to the world. If it is to have any worth it must offer a coherent viewpoint that allows people to discuss and explore what it will mean to move towards a human scale society. It is not the end of the story – a once and for all solution that we all know doesn't exist – but a beginning, a way of promoting the kind of debate that is necessary if language is to achieve the clarity and precision that will lead to widespread change. Like magnetising our piece of iron, stroking the electrons into alignment, the more effort that goes into the process, the stronger it becomes. What starts off as an inert lump of metal is transformed into a source of power that can affect everything around it.

The six values set out below mark out the boundaries of the territory we are calling the Human Scale. They do not attempt to explain or define the concept rigorously, but rather hint at its complexity, allowing individuals and groups to debate – and thereby understand and internalise – what it might mean to turn their backs on what is and set off in a different direction entirely.

THE HUMAN SCALE VALUES

RELATIONSHIPS
~ based on mutuality ~

COMMUNITIES
~ based on love and personal responsibility ~

LOCAL DECISION-MAKING
~ based on consensus ~

LOCAL FOOD/LOCAL WORK/LOCAL EXCHANGE/LOCAL ENERGY
~ based on creativity and sustainability ~

IDENTIFICATION WITH PLACE
~ based on oneness with nature ~

LIVING WITH UNCERTAINTY
~ based on spirituality -

Relationships – Based on Mutuality

We are so used to talking about power as one of the basic dimensions of human society that it may come as something of a surprise to see no mention of the word. That is because power is a form of relationship. To talk of power effectively depersonalises the transaction. If I have power over you then I can effectively ignore you. I may have to go through the pretence of listening to you but, if I have sufficient power, I can and will ignore you. In a world that is moving ever faster, I may not even be aware that I am doing so. Our freedoms inevitably depend on our relationship to others and it is in that balance between self and other that the nature of the social contract is defined. Tyranny and slavery are two ends of the same continuum.

In trying to achieve mutuality in relationships I am accepting that your point of view is as valid and important as mine. I can't ignore you and have to come to some accommodation with you. That doesn't mean that every transaction has to be equal (our exchange may be merely diverting for you, but life-enhancing to me), but it does mean that, in my relations with you, I have to take you into account. It also implies that, over all, we are looking at relationships that are based on give and take, rather than just give or take.

How might relationships based on mutuality be characterised? Put very simply, mutuality recognises that, if I want the freedom to pursue my own goals, then I must extend that privilege to you in equal measure. Paradoxically, that acknowledgement appears to restrict my freedom because, if I am sensitive to your aspirations, I cannot simply do as I wish, and I certainly should not be doing anything that diminishes your chances of realising your self. And the same applies to you, of course.

This apparent dilemma results from the fact that, from an individual point of view, freedom and equality are polar opposites. I can't have my cake and eat it. If I want the freedom to do what I want when I want, I have to assume that everyone else will be doing the same and only the strong will prevail. If I want protecting from the dangers inherent in that approach, I have to accept limitations on my freedom of action. As always it is a question of where the balance lies.

In the West we have developed a very particular view of the freedom/equality debate, namely an acceptance that, providing I don't actively do anyone harm (and that tends to be increasingly defined legalistically as we have seen), I am free to please myself. Lip service may be paid to equality, but we live in a meritocracy and bow down to the god of freedom. Perhaps because of its communist overtones, equality is seen as an unreasonable restriction of freedom, depriving people of their creativity and ability to be themselves. Thus, political correctness attempts to promote equality in an impersonal world, but only in the narrow sense of giving everyone equal access to the freedom to do as they please.

It is an essentially individualistic world view in which the needs of the other are largely abstract. This tendency is reinforced by the nature of our increasingly global society; we use an abstract medium of exchange (money) and the other person in any transaction is likely to be someone we can't possibly see or know (i.e. another abstraction). In these circumstances it is perhaps not surprising that there is so much exploitation and inequality in the world today; we not only don't have to confront the consequences of our actions, we are effectively immune from them.

One of the reasons that we are rarely entirely happy with the choices we make derives from this detachment from consequences. The apparently endless vistas of options that face us (limited only by our ability to pay) all seem equally attractive. To select one means abandoning the others and there is an inevitable sense of loss. Only by understanding the consequences of our actions for others can we take what we consider to be the "right" decision, which then produces a sense of certainty that allows other possibilities to be abandoned without regret. We are still free to make the "wrong" choice but, in the long run, to do so is likely to cause us harm. Freedom is never absolute. By being sheltered from the consequences of our actions (lacking feedback loops) we are being denied the option of acting responsibly: we are effectively being infantilised.

Although a desire for mutuality can come to inform all our relationships (by trying to understand the nature of the transactions that result from our desire to drink coffee produced elsewhere in the world, for example), it can really thrive only in relatively stable networks. Only in such a context can the contradictions inherent in the opposites self/other and freedom/equality be resolved. In such settings it is possible to imagine the freedom to do as I please becoming the freedom to explore who I am – and thereby grow and become stronger as an individual. Freedom in the first sense is limited only by my ability to pay for my pleasure and to hell with the consequences, in the second only by the number of people around me who are prepared to assist me on my journey and my expanding awareness of my impact on those others.

Other people become important and, if I want them to support and help me become myself, I must offer them the same opportunity. Indeed, true growth and development are unlikely to occur without that implicit mutuality because there is a sense in which we must all grow together if any of us are to grow at all. In other words, freedom and equality, rather than being contradictory, now complement and reinforce each other. It is a virtuous circle that not only leads to people who are more in touch with themselves and their potentialities, but who can express themselves for the benefit of the wider community. And that is because of the appearance of a new factor in the equation, which can be called love.

Love is a way of describing the energy that is present when people feel a strong sense of identification with, and commitment to, one another. It is the medium through which the self/other, freedom/equality oppositions can be resolved, creating the social glue that helps people adhere to one another and providing the goodwill and fellow feeling needed to overcome the inherently selfish nature of our beings. Trust is also more likely to be present in these circumstances, allowing people to be open and honest with one another, while being at the same time sensitive to each other's vulnerabilities. The fact that there is so little love of this kind in the world today is another measure of how serious the situation is.

But Love is a fragile flower and has to be nurtured carefully.

Communities – Based on Love and Personal Responsibility

The word *community* comes from the Latin *communis*, common; the suffix -ity denoting a quality or condition. Thus *community* means literally *being in common*. We bemoan the loss of community spirit and look back to some golden age that never actually existed to hide the fact that we have all but lost the ability to be in community – to be in common – with one another. We have become afraid of that commitment and sense of obligation and look to others for leadership, hoping thereby to avoid having to openly engage with others. We claim our rights and avoid our responsibilities.

Remember those people of long ago who gathered in dusty Greek marketplaces and debated issues of mutual concern until there was nothing more to say and then cast their vote? To avoid that responsibility would have appalled them and would have been seen as the very antithesis of citizenship. It would have demonstrated a lack of commitment to the polis that fell just short of treason.

And what about the fifty-five delegates to the American Constitutional Convention who spent from May to September in 1787, four months of almost daily meeting, thrashing out the details of an entirely new form of government that they hoped would ensure the survival of the fledgling experiment that had been launched only eleven years earlier with the Declaration of Independence? It is hard to imagine such examples of shared civic responsibility in our own times, nor the open-ended nature of the process. We are more used to decisions being taken elsewhere, of deals being done behind closed doors and no one being prepared to say exactly what they mean. We don't feature in this landscape and, anyway, we don't have time. Let them get on with it and we'll make hay while the sun shines. In that context looking after Number One begins to make sense. But the sun isn't going to shine for ever and, as soil in which to plant the seeds that might change the world, it doesn't look too promising.

By contrast, community depends on every individual's contribution. It is a collection of real people interacting in meaningful relationships rather than a list of names and addresses. To work, it requires that each member accepts their responsibility to participate to the full in the common enterprise and to acknowledge that their contribution is not fixed or defined but will vary according to the needs of the community as a whole and involve the full range of an individual's talents and resources. The more successful a community is at harnessing the skills of its members to meet the ever changing and varied circumstances it faces, the more fulfilled the individuals who compose it will be. Everyone benefits from a community that is thriving.

In that sense it is a very different animal to the kind of organisations that we are all part of and which we instinctively accept as "normal"; where roles are ascribed in a once and for all fashion that defines and limits the contribution that in individual can make, and where the fruits of success are rarely shared equitably amongst the membership. That is because a community is organic in nature, adapting instinctively to a changing environment, while an organisation is mechanistic and depends on hierarchical decision-making systems to change direction. To demonstrate this difference it is worth contrasting some of the attributes of both -

Community	Organisation
Emphasises relationships	Emphasises roles
Primacy of negotiation	Primacy of rules/procedures
Assumes co-operation	Assumes conflict
Emphasises responsibilities	Emphasises rights
Emphasises difference	Emphasises uniformity
Based on trust	Based on suspicion
Based on mutuality	Based on power
Based on personal talents	Based on position
Emphasising equality/consensus	Emphasising hierarchy/authority
Relationships based on covenant	Relationships based on contract

It should be noted that these qualities mainly reflect polar opposites and neither community nor organisation is at the extreme, rather they *tend* towards one pole rather than the other. As was suggested earlier there is a balance between order and chaos and how that is achieved in practice will inevitably reflect both ends of the spectrum of possibilities. Thus, both community and organisation will have elements of order and chaos in their make up, but it is in their overall orientation and emphases that the differences become marked and suggest why community is inherently more life-enhancing than organisation. community obviously requires organisation to survive but that is not its reason for existing.

The word *covenant* sums up that shift in emphasis. A covenant is a set of principles based directly on and derived from values such as those of the Human Scale already proposed. The choice of words and phrases it contains will reflect the interests and priorities of each community (i.e. although the values may be common, the covenants struck may differ in emphasis) and provide a reference point for all decision-making, both individual and collective.

In one sense a covenant bears some similarities to the mission statements so beloved of the corporate world. The differences are telling, however. A mission statement is imposed on people rather than involving them freely in its genesis – so they fail to understand its significance and ignore, or pay it lip service. It is not actually based on the fundamental values of the organisation – which can be summed up as being the need to survive in a hostile economic climate: individuals seek to better themselves at the expense of others and, for the business as a whole, the bottom line rules: everything else can and will be sacrificed to maintain profitability. In other words, there is a fundamental mismatch between the direction being signposted by the mission statement and what people are doing in practice. That is not a covenant.

An organisation exists for a specific and limited purpose and it sets about achieving its goals by trying to anticipate every aspect of its functioning. From the raw materials (plastics, metals, information, etc.) that it transforms into something else, to the people who work those changes and the way they approach the task, from the electricity bill to the coffee vending machine, everything is defined by contract. Nothing is left to chance because, only in that way, can the bottom line be calculated with any certainty. And that, at the end of the day, is what counts.

Once an organisation has tied down the parameters within which it is trying to operate it can move forward with confidence.

In a community, on the other hand, confidence comes, not from having everything circumscribed and limited (although that will happen to some degree), but through the knowledge that problems have been successfully overcome before. If you think about it, there is little point in a community trying to cover all the angles, because it doesn't have a single purpose, beyond the all-embracing one of coping with all that life may throw at it. It has to face the unknown, and to do that it depends on an open-ended covenant between its members rather than the straitjacket of contract that limits rather than liberates energy. Put simply, a covenant is an agreement based on mutual trust, goodwill and a desire to work towards a shared goal or vision. It is a joint commitment to set out on a journey that has no end, whose route is uncertain, and where successful strategies in the past may prove wanting in the future. What sustains people is their shared vision and the belief that what they are doing is important.

Because it is organic in nature, a community will evolve differently from an organisation. An organism is self-regulating. That is to say that it responds instinctively to a change in circumstances. If someone drinks more than they're accustomed to, the bladder automatically speeds up its functioning and produces the desire to urinate. It doesn't require the intervention of other organs or of consciousness itself. An organisation, on the other hand, would deal with similar, relatively small-scale changes by passing the problem up and down the management chain until an interim solution is found (an additional person drafted into the department in question) and the matter can be left to the annual review and resources reallocated on a more permanent basis if the problem persists.

Gentle exercise has an impact on all the body's organs and increasing fitness can turn a couch potato into someone capable of running a marathon; the organisational response to a perceived lack of fitness – increasing competitiveness – is radical surgery on otherwise healthy component parts: people are made redundant. Extending the analogy to communities it is possible to see how they grow organically. Change may occur in one individual (cell) but, if sustained, that will have an impact on all the other members and both the nature and potential of the community will have been changed as a consequence. That just doesn't happen in an organisation where, no matter how gifted or talented one person may be, their ability to change the way the whole functions is limited by their ability to reach those at the top who hold the power.

In the mutually reinforcing kind of growth possible in a community, the result is both a clearer and deeper sense of the others involved, but also a deeper and clearer sense of self. It is the environment in which the balance between self and other is most likely to be achieved and to engender the sense of love that binds people to one another, and provides the impetus for yet more growth and development. It is another example of a virtuous circle.

It is easy to see why personal qualities become so important and why authority and leadership will be vested in individuals who earn that trust, rather than through occupying positions in a hierarchy or being members of a family who have traditionally held such roles. In this sense leadership is more about responsibility than about power, and carries the weight of obligation to those who have placed their trust in someone rather than privilege. Authority in a community is offered to people rather than taken by them and reflects a general perception that, through the integrity and wisdom of their own person, they somehow embody the aspirations of everyone. It need not even require formal recognition, but come naturally as others listen to what they say and follow their example. And the wonder is that a community can have many leaders of this kind – each possessing qualities that are fitted to a different aspect of collective functioning – without descending into chaos.

A group of people coming together does not ensure a sense of community. That requires effort and time. And there is always the danger of stagnation, even death.

Put simply, the quality of its decision-making determines whether a community thrives or declines.

Local Decision-making Based on Consensus

There are many ways of making decisions:-

- authoritarian

- consultative

- participatory

- consensual

We are dealing, once again, with polar opposites – authoritarian (one individual making decisions) on the one hand, and consensual (everyone being involved) on the other, with consultative and participatory in between on the spectrum. As with all polar opposites it is extremely difficult (and unhealthy) to operate at the extremes. Even the most paranoid and ruthless of despots rely on the advice of those around them, and to involve everyone in every little decision would be recipe for chaos and probably lead to violence. The trick is to choose the most appropriate decision-making approach to deal with the problem in hand.

It is also important to recognise that reason alone will not always yield the best answers. We occupy a moral universe as well as a physical one, and the same rules do not necessarily apply to both. As we have seen, our development as human beings determines our orientation to the world. It is an incredibly complex mix of influences, prohibitions and drives that we can never be wholly conscious of – and therefore test against some objective yardstick of reason. Indeed, looked at from an organic perspective, it would actually be undesirable to do so, as the organism is quite capable of taking care of itself without interference from the higher functions such as consciousness. For the most part we respond to reality holistically, that is from the whole of our being. There are certainly problems with such a way of dealing with life, but reason is likely to play only a minor role in resolving them (for example, as we consciously try to do things differently). We are all aware that our attitudes and emotions fluctuate, sometimes with bewildering speed, and inevitably contain many tensions and contradictions as well as embracing all the Freudian defences against psychic stress – sublimation, projection, denial rationalisation, etc. But we also bring many positive features into play in our interactions with others, such as empathy, intuition, an awareness of our own feelings, etc. and it is in the deployment of these in the context of a network of secure and stable relationships (a community) that we are most likely to be able to confront and change those aspects of ourselves that cause difficulties to us and those around us. That is how we find our way around the moral maze.

By contrast, the scientific method has proved pre-eminent in unravelling the mysteries of the physical world. It is essentially a conscious, detached process, a careful study of phenomena uncontaminated by the bias and error perceived to be inherent in the unconscious, with the results endlessly replicable by others. Over time, all reasonable people will conclude that the findings are valid. It is a powerful technique but not one that is applicable in all situations. For a start, it depends on an ability to take complex entities apart, study them and then apply the conclusions reached to the whole. In the jumbled confusion that is the real world that step-by-step approach simply isn't possible; decisions have to be taken in the here and now.

The scientific method also depends on there being sufficient data to allow patterns and trends to emerge through ongoing experiment, and for those same conditions to be available elsewhere so that their significance can be independently verified. Much of what happens in the moral universe is a one-off that can never be replicated in its entirety (how can we know what would have happened if the Coalition had decided not to invade Iraq?). Many of the critical moments (both highs and lows) in an individual's life are singularities that carry an intensity that may remain with that person for the rest of their life, but which are difficult to compare in any meaningful sense with the experiences of others (they have to be accepted or rejected on the basis of our own personal orientation and knowledge).

Another way of posing this dilemma is to recognise that not all problems have a resolution that everyone that approaches them rationally can agree on. As Schumacher suggested in *A Guide for the Perplexed*[1], the problems that scientists typically encounter in the physical universe are convergent in nature (over time they converge on a generally agreed solution). But such problems are only part of the story. There is also a category of problem that is essentially divergent and that tends to produce a polarisation of views if approached from a purely rational point of view. These problems are most commonly found in the moral universe and concern the decisions we make in our daily lives. They become to the fore when we are asked to make judgements about what is important in life (what should we do with paedophiles/asylum seekers/murderers? should scientists clone human embryos? should citizens be allowed to own guns?); they naturally engage our emotions and belief systems (our assumptions about the world we live in that can't ultimately be proved) as well as our reason – in other words, our whole beings. They are also likely to be found in the complex, interrelated arena of public policy, and typically produce either laissez-faire or interventionist responses (do you get cars out of city centres by banning them, or by letting things get so bad that people literally vote with their feet?). Reason is here used to justify a committed stance rather than explore the world from a neutral, detached one.

This tendency for divergence shouldn't be a surprise once we recognise that the moral universe is essentially bi-polar in nature, and that coping with its tensions is about maintaining an ever shifting balance rather than finding a once and for all solution. Applying reason in such circumstances inevitably produces divergence because of the tendency for any argument to automatically sheer off towards the extremes as we attempt rationally and reasonably to convince an increasingly entrenched opponent of the error of their ways. As the distance separating the two positions begins to grow, reason is finally thrown out of the window as both sides try to destroy the other to maintain the purity of their (rational) position. It is the basis of our adversarial systems of politics and justice and, as we have seen, it no longer works in a complex, atomistic world.

Finally, the great strength of science is its ability to predict events in the physical world and we wouldn't be human if we didn't yearn for the same kind of certainty in the moral universe. Reason holds out the promise that, if only we could rid ourselves of our prejudices, blind spots and emotional baggage, we could predict the future and everything would be perfect. It is a fantasy, of course, and unattainable if only because, in a bi-polar world, every action produces a reaction; the more extreme the action, the more extreme the reaction. Perfection is asking for imperfection to come along and give it a bloody nose. And how the reaction comes is usually unforeseeable; it is called a random event.

Despite the almost miraculous homogeneity and apparent predictability of humanity in the mass, there are always individuals and groups who are acting against the prevailing mood (not necessarily consciously). Whether it is by ignoring laws, or campaigning actively against them, the effect is usually marginal, a bit like an itch on the collective skin. Every once in a while, however, the irritation erupts. Individuals and groups are thrust into the limelight and assume a symbolic importance as issues, real or imagined, are elevated to the level of a national scandal. A bit of the world is changed and, while it can be argued that it would have happened sooner or later, it is impossible to demonstrate that in practice (it is a singularity and we cannot re-run time). How the problem actually emerges will influence what happens subsequently and, in that sense, both the event and its outcome are inherently unpredictable.

9/11 is an example of a random event that changed the world. Even if you could have predicted that something like it was going to happen, could you have begun to guess at the impact it would have?

Reality then is far too complex to predict and, however reasonable our decisions appear at the time, we cannot be sure that their result will be positive. Put like that, it sounds as though there is little point in even trying to anticipate and plan for the future. A central thesis of this book has been the significance of decision-making systems in determining how successful a society will be in responding to the challenges it faces. How can we plan for the future and why should Human Scale societies be any better at making decisions than our existing ones?

First, as with everything else we have discussed so far, it is a question of scale. The closer we are to the events we are trying to anticipate, the more likely we are to get it right. I know roughly what I will be doing half an hour from now because the decisions

I am taking now tend in that direction. I can also make a pretty good guess about what the other members of my immediate family will be up to. Trying to anticipate what someone I've never met might be doing a year from now is obviously more difficult, if not impossible. And yet that is precisely what governments are attempting to do when they plan legislation that may be in force for decades and influence the lives of many millions of people. Looked at from this perspective, such an approach seems inherently flawed.

We also need to be flexible enough to be able to change tack if the circumstances suggest our original assumptions were wrong. To persist with a barbecue in pouring rain just because the weather forecast assured us it would be hot and sunny would be viewed as highly eccentric behaviour, and yet our cumbersome legislative and political machines produce some uncanny resemblances to just that scenario. Feedback loops are the way organisms adjust to changing conditions and, once again, the more immediate they are, the more likely the animal is to adopt an appropriate strategy.

The conclusions are irresistible: small groupings of people who are in touch with one another and what is going on around them, have a shared set of values and a covenant that specifies their joint priorities, and who can respond quickly and positively to changes that occur in their moral and physical environments, are more likely to react successfully to any challenges they face. But aren't small groups, are prone simply to collapse under the weight of trying to agree anything? Isn't chaos the most likely outcome? That danger is present in all human relations, and trying to pretend it doesn't exist won't make it go away.

We must also accept that many people see the anonymity of mass society as providing the best protection against hostility, prejudice and violence, and view the prospect of opening themselves to others with genuine fear and distrust. The reality, however, is that humanity en masse can be fickle and, while being out of sight and out of mind may be a successful strategy for long periods of time, the crowd can turn with terrifying speed and consequences. When it does no one is safe. At least in small groupings there is the opportunity – indeed, as we shall see, the

110

requirement – to address difference and, if resolution proves impossible, there is less likelihood of physical ill-use. To paraphrase Leopold Kohr in *The Breakdown of Nations*[2], a Hitler can do less damage in a small community than at the head of a vast nation.

To understand how these problems can be avoided, we must recognise that organisms have purpose (which may simply be to survive and replicate themselves) and that the internal organs and cells each have a function within that overall scheme (which they independently and unconsciously perform). In human terms, the community can be viewed as the organism and its purpose as a shared vision about what is important and worth achieving. That shared vision (the covenant) will inform what the individual cells (people) do as they go about their different functions and thereby contribute to achieving those goals. It follows that the greater the clarity of the shared vision, the more likely it is that the social magnet will be fully charged and create the conditions for the component cells to work successfully and creatively together.

The only way that a shared vision can be achieved is through consensus – bringing together everyone who has a stake in the outcome and reaching an agreement that all are happy with. Consensus is not about compromise that somehow papers over the cracks between different, entrenched positions, because everyone emerges from the process changed. No individual or group can be in control because, in choosing to enter the process, each is accepting that the outcome is uncertain. People can come with firm views, but there must be an acceptance that where each of us is today is the result of the complex matrix of experiences described in Chapter 5, which create inevitable biases, even prejudices, in our outlook.

They must face the different but equally valid perspectives of others in an open minded way that will lead inevitably to a reassessment of their own position, resulting in changes, however slight, that may result in deeper understanding or even a Divine Right of Kings Moment where they can see another reality altogether. There can be no deals done in advance, no hidden agendas and no place for manipulation, just a confidence that a way forward can be found that will embrace everyone's altering point of view. The process is all-important and it is about listening to others and clarifying what is being said. Along the way, the meaning of individual words will be explored and, as a result, language subtly changes its meaning until everyone shares a common perception of the issues and their potential resolution; the individual electrons are gradually being aligned and a magnetic charge created.

It is time-consuming but, if we want good decision-making to replace the spreading morass of knee jerk, ill-conceived responses to the latest storm in a teacup, it is time worth taking. And, miraculously, it is a process that builds strength, both at the individual and community level, the more practised we become. Much of the time is spent, not on the detail of the issues being discussed, but in trying to understand one another as people, where we are coming from and what makes us take a particular stance (an entrenched position often conceals a long-standing and deep-seated anxiety of which the person may be unaware). That is an opportunity for personal growth, both through receiving feedback about ourselves and our contribution, but also through sharing our perceptions of others in a way that they can accept and take on board. Sensitivity to the other and an ever-deepening identification with them become the order of the day. Paradoxically, it is often the least sure, those who do not offer clear opinions, but who are silent, even withdrawn, who hold the key to such change. They are unsure and, for that very reason, helping them to resolve the conflicts that their uncertainty reveals is likely to be of benefit to all. Those who speak most frequently or coherently are often least helpful in reaching consensus.

For such intimacy to exist suggests relatively small groups of people coming together over time. There needs to be experimentation before the optimum size for such groupings will be understood, but anywhere from thirty to one hundred and fifty (the inhabitants of a street, for example) suggests itself as being small enough for genuine dialogue to be possible, while large enough to produce meaningful decisions for the community. When neighbouring communities need to come together over specific issues it may be possible for everyone to be involved, but for gatherings of several communities, or local, regional and global assemblies (see page 133/134) representation will be necessary.

When all else fails, having a shared value base allows the space to explore issues dispassionately by asking the question "ok, so we can't agree the way forward, what does our value base suggest is the most likely route towards achieving our vision?" Looked at in this way there is less likelihood of people feeling they have been backed into a win/lose situation and for a "third way", incorporating the best of the opposing viewpoints, to emerge.

Consensus is also the means by which we achieve a balance between retaining personal responsibility – being involved in and accepting responsibility for decisions that are made collectively – and trusting others to get on and do things appropriately. We give others the authority to act on our behalf by agreeing the parameters within which such authority can be exercised (and by whom) and the manner in which the individuals or group so charged remains accountable (which may include consultation and participation). That is best done consensually, through the evolving of a shared language that will ensure that the magnetising process continues to work once everyone is getting on with their daily lives. Inevitably, over time, that charge will seep away and, even when there is little change in the community, there will be a need for regular consensual meetings to ensure that the vision and the common language in which it is expressed still resonate. That necessity will be even greater if internal or external factors are creating a pressure for change.

A community, then, uses all forms of decision-making, but in an integrated way that ensures that what is agreed consensually is achieved in the most effective way. What is done is transparent and open to sensitive questioning by anyone, thereby ensuring that the feedback loops so necessary for healthy adaptation to changing circumstances are in place and functioning.

Local Food/Local Work/Local Energy/Local Exchange Based on Creativity and Sustainability

Approximately one-third of all the energy we use in the West goes on transport, and the bulk of that is in the form of hydrocarbon fuels that produce greenhouse gases. The internal combustion engine is doing enormous environmental damage and, for that reason alone, we should be putting the emphasis on staying local in all aspects of our daily lives. In America, for example, urban sprawl and the clinical split between work and home has led to a complete dependence on the use of a car – it is simply the only option (being out of work means you can't afford a car, means you can't find work – it is a vicious circle). Our addiction to being able to move about quickly and cheaply means that we think nothing of getting in the car to go round the corner. We no longer keep fit by walking, but by driving round to a gym and using expensive machinery (which takes yet more energy to construct).

There is another, perhaps even more fundamental, reason for weaning ourselves from our dependence on oil. It is running out (see Appendix 1 – pages 165-172)! Not only that, but demand for the stuff is increasing as China and India seek promotion to the premier division of the economic league. With consumption now far exceeding the discovery of new reserves, the phenomenon of "peak oil" is upon us – the point at which production peaks and begins to decline no matter what the demand. When that happens – and many analysts believe it is happening right now – the impact on the world economy and the flow of consumer goods we take for granted will be disastrous.

Giving up our cars won't be easy. Our addiction is not due solely to the convenience that personalised transport offers, the car is also symbolic. In a society where no one knows anyone else, the car has become a potent token of self, giving out a range of messages; from understated affluence to in-your-face wealth, from being on trend to blatant sexual display. Above all cars are part of the swirling sea of fashion that define who we are to others, who can only judge by such external appearances. As such, they are of the moment, evanescent, and have little connection with the real world.

Our, often unconscious, hopes and desires about the lifestyles we aspire to, and how we would like to be seen, are artificially created and fuelled by endless makeover programmes and our unprecedented access to role models whose fame is a reflection of our need for style icons rather than any more concrete talent. We are encouraged to live a dream and, if we are usually disappointed with how our lives actually are, that's because we aren't trying hard enough. Switch to a different manufacturer, but above all else – spend, spend, spend. Meanwhile, pollution continues to increase, more and more of our countryside disappears under tarmac, and our streets resemble parking lots. The car is king and it is time for a Divine Right of Kings Moment.

But there are still other, even more pressing reasons for going local. As suggested in Chapter Two, the way supermarkets source food is inherently unsafe and unsustainable. Transporting animals huge distances for slaughter inevitably induces stress which is known to affect the quality of meat. Abattoirs are large-scale enterprises run on factory lines where animal welfare is not a prime consideration. To minimise the risks of cross-contamination, complex systems of tracking both live animals and carcasses are necessary and, as continuing health scares testify, are not always effective. The unrelenting pressure to keep costs down leads to agri-business and monoculture and, in the case of cereal and other crops, the long-term viability of the soil is being endangered. To add insult to injury, the mass produced, ready-made meals that result from these perilous practices would be hopelessly bland where it not for the impressive range of additives and flavourings (mainly artificial) necessary to make them palatable.

Food is fundamental to life and good food to a good life. And it isn't hard to achieve. If you think about it, food is a renewable source of energy. Provided the soil is nurtured properly, it will go on meeting our needs for ever. If we all grew our own food the only costs would be the time we devoted to the task and the tools we needed to do it. Because we *don't* grow what we eat, we have to pay for it, but we have been kidded into believing that food is essentially marginal to our budgets and can be treated like any other commodity (a computer is the equivalent of so many kilos of potatoes). Not only that, our demand for fresh food throughout the year means we have lost touch with the seasons themselves and the natural rhythms that underpin existence. As a consequence, we no longer value food properly. Instead, we see cheapness as a right, allowing us to consume all the non-edible goodies we feel are even more essential to life.

115

Only by reasserting a local dimension to the production of food can we hope to reverse these trends. To be able to exercise our own personal responsibility in this key area, we need to reconnect with the rhythms and cycles of the seasons and accept the limitations that they impose. That implies becoming involved in the processes of growing, harvesting, transporting and marketing the produce we consume. Buying direct from farmers through farmers' markets and supporting greengrocers and butchers who source their produce locally are both starting points but, ultimately, communities need to take responsibility for accessing as much food locally as possible, thereby ensuring its provenance and quality. To buy locally reared beef in Kidwelly, South Wales, for example, may still mean the meat has travelled up to 500 miles (the cattle are transported to North Wales for slaughter, back to South Wales for processing and packaging, off to a regional distribution centre in Gloucester and then on to the local supermarket)[3].

Local in this context is a relative term. Cities with millions of inhabitants obviously cannot support their populations from within their boundaries (although much more could be produced than is at present) and have to look to their hinterlands. From this perspective it is possible to imagine communities creating ongoing links with a range of farmers, even negotiating what crops or livestock are to be produced and in what quantities. They may even provide labour at key stages in the process, helping to keep costs down (and thus providing a genuine exchange *between* communities). Not everything can be produced in this way – some regions are better suited to some products than others – but becoming involved will provide a sense of the true costs of growing food and make us more realistic in how we access foodstuffs that cannot be grown locally.

Once food is available it has to be prepared and cooked. Not everyone has skills or interest in this area, but those who do could produce batches of ready-cooked meals that are then chilled or frozen and exchanged within the local community. We are beginning to see the emergence of local work, that is to say activities that are undertaken by, and for the benefit of, the community. One of the problems with work as defined by large-scale organisations is that only those skills that are of use to them are fully utilised. Based on the benefits (to the structure) of a strictly utilitarian division of labour, these are by definition limited; we become specialists and spend the majority of our time focused on a single, narrow aspect of a task that is artificial and largely meaningless in the wider scheme of things. At the same time, in a world dominated by technology, we increasingly need other specialists to help us survive because we can no longer repair even the simplest of machines. Certain aspects of our personality become overdeveloped while we become totally de-skilled in others.

Work, as an activity, should have two functions for the individual. It should provide a challenge, during which something is completed or achieved – either for ourselves or for others – and, as a consequence, our competence and sense of worth is reinforced. In that sense we are what we do. When work is freely chosen it is perhaps the single most important way in which we explore ourselves and the potential we embody. Humans have endless curiosity and a desire to experience new things, and we need ongoing opportunities to develop skills and knowledge if we are not to stagnate and die creatively. When money is the sole reason given by many people for going to work, it is hardly surprising that they see what they squeeze into their spare time – their hobbies and voluntary activity – as what truly defines them. Wouldn't society be better off if it could harness this energy the whole week, rather than have it reluctantly given to paid employment?

And when money, and what it can buy, is the only tangible outcome of paid work – and the only way to get yet more of it is through promotion – it is hardly surprising that enormous amounts of time, energy and skill go into careers as being the only measure available of self-worth. The fact that a moment's reflection tells you that very few make it to the top only adds to the frenzied desire to be one of them, no matter what damage it may do to oneself and others in the process. All the ugliness of corporate politics, cutting corners, sharp practice and inevitable burn-out are implicit in a system that doesn't acknowledge the true importance of work to the individual and their sense of who they are.

Local work, by contrast, recognises and rewards individual skill and accomplishment. Almost any activity that you can think of – from joinery to cheese-making, from dress-making to growing food – requires more skill when undertaken on a small scale. That isn't to reject the role of machinery – even high-tech machinery – in production. It is rather a recognition that, to compete effectively in global markets, processes have to be large-scale and the function of mechanisation is thus to produce standardised components (in terms of size, shape and quality) at the lowest possible price, which inevitably reduces the amount of human input required and channels their activity. The investment is in the machinery not the human being; local work reassesses that balance by putting skill back into the equation. Technology becomes *appropriate* to the task it is performing.

Just as we can make choices about the kind of food we eat and where it comes from, so we can opt to support local work. All that is required is information about what is available locally. The abilities of particular individuals will be easier to gauge (marking the end of the cowboy worker) and, over time, local knowledge will extend those skills and interests. It will be easier to discuss and shape the product or service to both parties satisfaction. Face-to-face contact will increase trust and remove the need for the full panoply of insurance, health and safety, environmental health, specialist lawyers, etc., etc. to protect against anything going wrong (although communities need to create mechanisms for dealing with disputes, they will be human in scale and person-centred). And because there will not be the same imperative to work full-time on a single activity there will be the opportunity for each of us to develop in many ways over a lifetime. At any moment an individual may be passing on their methods to others in their community (and teaching in this sense would be classed as local work) and learning new skills from someone else.

All work requires energy and, with oil running out in the fore-seeable future, there is an ongoing debate about what the energy economy of the future might look like[4]. On the one hand there is the nuclear option and, on the other, the development of what are called renewables (using wind, solar, biomass, etc.). This book is not the place to discuss whether nuclear power stations are actually sustainable (there is an argument that suggests that, with so much energy consumed in their planning and construction – energy derived, at present, from fossil fuels – it can take up to ten years of their operational life to pay back the carbon they have emitted – hardly a quick fix in the battle to reduce energy consumption), but their basic nature will clearly reinforce our current centralised, authoritarian ways of organising society and make the kind of Human Scale communities we have been looking at more difficult to achieve. The implications of the best way to produce energy when oil runs out are thus profound because they will impact on our ability to devise the coherent decision-making systems on which our future depends.

Most electricity grids in the developed world are top-down. They distribute the electricity generated at a few locations (power stations) to a myriad of consumers, balancing demand by drawing on the supplies available to the grid as a whole. It is not a particularly efficient system in terms of energy loss inherent in the process. An alternative is to stand the model on its head and see each house as both a consumer from and a *contributor* to a local grid (the technology is available in the form of photovoltaic cells, small-scale wind turbines, biomass stoves and ground source heat pumps: in the future it might be achieved more effectively through the storage of hydrogen) supported by a range of medium-scale, renewable generation systems situated locally (at present wind turbines are sited for purely commercial reasons and, to maximise return, this inevitably means building them big, putting several together and siting them in positions where they can't be ignored; communities wouldn't be constrained by the same economic considerations and could elect to choose less conspicuous if less efficient sites).

It is a bottom-up solution to our energy crisis with regional and national grids providing back-up to iron out any temporary fluctuations in the local grids. Electricity is power and community-owned systems of generation would be a visible and apt symbol of local empowerment.

Home, we are told, is where the heart is and, by concentrating on our local neighbourhoods, we are more likely to build up the kind of long-term, mutual relationships that will foster communities based on love and personal responsibility and enable local decisions based on consensus to be taken. Local food, work and energy will be cornerstones of this new focus, but they will not be possible without local exchange. If we are to reward creativity and ensure that products are both needed and made to a standard that will ensure they last – thereby justifying the use of energy that went into creating them – we need to find ways of protecting local trade from the vagaries of the global economy.

Not only does the global marketplace encourage mass production that removes individual human creativity from the equation, it produces goods that people don't really need and that are quickly disposed of, and made in a way that takes little account of energy use over the life cycle of the product. Worse still, it takes the fulcrum of exchange away from the local community and places it far away in the boardrooms of corporate power where decisions, as we have seen, cannot take account of real human beings. As a consequence, communities, especially those dependent on only a few big employers, can be marginalised at the stroke of the corporate pen and, once on the scrap heap, there is usually no way back.

It is this dependence on a system over which local people have no control and which, by its very nature, is inherently arbitrary that local exchange seeks to overturn. Only by decoupling ourselves from an economic machine that replaces the essentially simple nature of human exchange with a voracious and escalating need for more of everything can we begin to stand against the tide that is remorselessly dragging us towards destruction. There will continue to be a place for trade between communities and around the world, but it will be from a position of robust local markets and based on systems of fair exchange.

How might this be achieved? Money, as we have seen, is a human construct and, as such, falls in the Divine Right of Kings Moment category of phenomena that appear god-given, but which can be changed or dispensed with altogether, almost at will. We are so used to having national currencies that they have come to define who we are, as the ongoing debate about Britain joining the Euro shows. In theory, there is no reason why both the Pound Sterling *and* the Euro shouldn't be used in parallel, retaining the supposed advantages of controlling one's own economic affairs while at the same time enjoying the benefits of using a single currency throughout much of Europe *and* being involved in monetary policy at that level as well.

Looked at from the other end of the scale there is nothing to stop a small group of people who regularly do things for each other agreeing their own informal exchange system – which might even include the issuing of tokens (money) – while still having access to conventional money. Many baby-sitting circles already work on this basis, but there is nothing that says the trans-actions should be limited to a single activity. Once that step is accepted we are well on the way to creating a viable, local monetary system. Examples of such parallel currencies are now commonplace (see page 155) with perhaps the most successful appearing in Latin America, where Creditos have been used as a medium of exchange by the poor to protect themselves from problems caused by unstable national currencies.

The issues that any monetary system faces are: who controls it, for whose benefit and what principles underpin the system of exchange? As we have seen, the global economy is effectively controlled by the banking system for its own benefit, and exchange is based on usury (the paying of unfair interest on loans) and free markets (which allows the strong to exploit the weak). Local exchange, by contrast, would be controlled by local people, for their own benefit, and would be based on the primacy of mutuality in relationships[5].

Local priorities would be agreed locally, with decisions about significant loans (investment in the future) taken by the commu-nity as a whole (or through mechanisms agreed consensually that would then be open to scrutiny by all). If one or more individuals wished to start an enterprise, for example, they would have to convince their community that it was not only viable but that it served some communal good. Once agreed, however, the project would have everyone's full backing and would be more likely to succeed as a consequence. There are costs associated with running such a system and, as with credit unions at present, a small amount of interest might be charged to cover the cost of running the service – but it could also be seen as part of the service provided by the community and funded through its own revenue-generating mechanisms (see below).

The importance of replacing free markets with what might be called mutual markets cannot be overemphasised. Free markets inevitably produce cheap, standardised articles that are aimed at a generalised audience rather than specific individuals; they also tend to amplify the gap between the haves and the have-nots. A mutual market will accentuate the link between individuals and the resulting product or service will reflect this, meaning that people will get what they actually want. A dialogue (feedback loop) can develop that will change the perception of both the producer and the customer through the course of the transaction. It will also be possible to factor in all the costs involved, from the natural resources used (and their cost in terms of replacement or recycling) to the machinery used to transform them and the impact that manufacture might have on the environment; all will be visible to the wider community and, by ensuring transparency in each transaction, people will be able to make decisions based on real knowledge.

But it will be in terms of how transactions are negotiated that the fundamental difference between free and mutual markets will be apparent. Under the present system, the only constraint on either buyer or seller is to get the best deal they can. Sometimes the buyer is in the stronger position, sometimes the seller but, in neither case are the consequences of the decisions we take an issue (or usually even known to the parties). If I buy a cheap piece of electrical equipment from a retailer because they are going bust, I am unlikely to give any thought at all to the circumstances that produced my good fortune. My personal responsibility in the transaction is very limited.

With relations based on mutuality, that lack of concern for the other would be unthinkable. That doesn't mean that I should continue to support someone in all circumstances, but it does mean that I should take time to understand the problem. Maybe someone else in the community is producing better-quality work in less time, maybe the particular skills on offer are no longer required. In those circumstances, I – and the wider community – have a responsibility to see if the individual can be helped to develop skills in other areas. As most people will be offering a range of talents in our local-market place this change of emphasis shouldn't prove too difficult, but it does highlight one further requirement for mutual markets – the basis of exchange should be fair.

If we are to value everyone equally (and to encourage their growth and development for the benefit of all) we need to ensure that their opportunities are not artificially limited. One of the iniquities of the present system is that people's access to a range of resources – from health care to education, from healthy food to good housing – depends on one thing, their wealth, and that bears no relation to their personal merits or their contribution to the community as a whole. The only fair basis for mutual exchange is to value everyone's contribution equally by starting from the principle that an hour of my time is worth the same as an hour of yours *no matter what we are both doing*. As we are all limited by the number of hours in the day, the only differential that can emerge will be a reflection of the fact that I am lazier than you – but it will never be as wide as the gap between rich and poor at present; and the nature of being part of a vibrant community is also likely to encourage me to want to play my part to the full!

Many more tasks than at present will be appropriately addressed through negotiations between people, and that will be another reflection of handing power back to local communities. Much of the current health care and educational monoliths can be dismantled in this way, with people making choices about whom they wish to engage with to discuss health matters or seek to learn from (this switch will, in turn, release the enormous amount of time and energy that are locked into these institutions and that have little direct impact on what they deliver in practice – another rich vein of people resources can be found in dismantling the legal and quasi-legal octopus whose tentacles now reach into every aspect of daily living and which will become redundant once face-to-face negotiations about disputes become commonplace).

Nevertheless, much will remain that will be communal in nature – looking after public spaces, collecting and recycling waste, local insurance schemes, etc. – and will have to be handled by the raising of local tithes (taxes), decisions regarding spending of which will be the responsibility of the whole community. These activities will become yet another source of local work and will require a range of skills that will allow everyone to play their part in ongoing upkeep of the social, physical and spiritual environment. Local money will keep circulating and, in the process, create tangible, lasting wealth.

An approach to food, work and energy that is based on systems of local, mutual exchange will begin the long process of learning how to live within our means that is so necessary if we are to step back from the precipice. It will not, in itself, meet all the needs of each individual in every community. Trade between communities – which might specialise in certain crafts or trades because of particular local resources or skills – will be an important part of the processes by which neighbouring communities, regions and eventually the whole world are tied together (for example, even in the Iron Age metals were mined in a few locations, rough worked on site and then traded over vast distances to be finished by local craftsmen). The principle of mutuality should still inform such transactions – because any other basis is potentially exploitative – and that suggests that such exchange will diminish the greater the distances between the trading partners.

Gandhi had a vision of an India, not of mega-cities, but of a confederation of interdependent villages and small towns; self-organising, sufficient communities, each having the skills and resources necessary for a simple but good life, and together making up a vibrant, caring and sustainable society. Now more than ever we need to be taking the steps to realise his dream.

Identification with Place Based on Oneness with Nature

We may be part of many communities – real and virtual – that enrich our lives, but there is only one community that can ultimately take responsibility for life – and that is the community of people who live on a particular piece of land; in other words, a unique geographical community. If they feel no need to identify with and nurture the earth beneath their feet, who will? And that is the point we have reached. We may be able to send people into space and cure illnesses that devastated previous generations, but it has been at the price of losing the connection with the ground of our being.

Only by coming together on the basis of mutuality, making important decisions consensually and taking responsibility for the work that is done locally can we hope to understand and integrate ourselves with the ultimate source of all life on this planet. Only then can we truly know who we are, both our potentialities and our limitations. By identifying completely with a piece of land – exploring its potentialities and limitations – we become part of the web of life that sustains us. We are no longer detached, objective beings trying to master our environment but equal, engaged participants in a process that we contribute to and take from in equal measure; that, ultimately, is the meaning of sustainability.

The healthier, more diverse and stronger that web, the healthier, more diverse and stronger will be our communities. From this recognition it is but a short step to the rediscovery of the old wisdom visible in local traditions of craftwork and the building techniques most appropriate to each local environment. Over time, a particular environment will come to shape what is produced from, as well as what is built on, it.

That will be a reflection of the nature of the wider landscape in which a community is located and, as well as a commitment to a particular piece of land, it will be natural to look outwards and identify with the surrounding countryside. In this context it is important to define what exactly it is that we are identifying with. A bio-region is distinguished by natural rather than human boundaries, a naturally self-contained area defined by its topography, its animals, plants, soil and climate, etc and bio-regionalism becomes the building blocks in any regional, national and global structures[6].

As we have seen, transactions between neighbouring communities, particularly in relation to food, will make people more sensitive to the assets available to them and their limitations. The same applies to natural resources such as water and recognising that joint planning and work will be necessary to ensure their long-term viability. A bio-region provides the context in which this cooperation can and should happen. It can be characterised by hills or mountains or by a particular river system, but those who inhabit it will recognise and celebrate its uniqueness. And through that identification they can also come to learn what it has to offer and the limitations that must not be passed if it is to continue to provide its bounty. In seeing it as a whole, and making a commitment to it, they are also likely to ensure that each of its constituent communities does not do anything that will impact unfavourably elsewhere. Having a variety of approaches in different regions of the world will be seen as a virtue and diversity will once more be valued. That is another ancient wisdom that we have almost entirely lost with our headlong rush towards uniformity and the implicit belief that everywhere is basically the same.

While the Earth is abundant, not all areas are equally favoured. Choosing or having to live in a particular place carries that implicit acceptance of limitation but, as we saw earlier, a sense of rightness is the way to counter the desire to keep all options open that is so characteristic of the world today. It is not reasonable to want everything, and that is another sign of how far we have travelled from a sense of balance in all things. It is axiomatic that communities exist in place as well as time and we should be satisfied with that, looking outside only for those things we cannot produce ourselves and which other people are willing to freely exchange with us.

Living With Uncertainty Based on Spirituality

Humans, as we have seen, are creatures of habit. Most of us are quite content if tomorrow is much like today and we organise our lives accordingly. It is one of our greatest weaknesses as a species. Another is believing that we have created a society that is in control of its destiny and that every day is getting better in every way – despite the evidence that, as our organisations become ever bigger and more complex, so do the problems we face. We like certainty and would rather avoid uncertainty, so we are complacent amidst the gathering storm.

Understanding that existence is inherently unpredictable and mysterious is thus the final dimension that we need to explore and become more sensitive to if we are to create successful Human Scale communities. Life is a process. Like a river, movement is its natural condition; it is always changing, never still. Both the river and your life may appear the same each time you observe them, but they never are; which is why change, when it happens, invariably takes us by surprise – a tree falling into the river and spoiling a favourite view, or a sudden illness. Both appear as random events, without meaning, but both are an integral and inevitable part of the river's or individual's story; one cannot be fully understood without the other.

Once we accept that change is as much a part of the fabric of creation as stability, and that order is always on the point of collapsing into chaos, we are beginning to open ourselves to uncertainty. And in that process we become more sensitive to the cues that give the great drama of life its illusion of permanence. We become less distracted by the artificial creations – laws, contracts, working routines, deadlines, etc., etc. – with which humans have surrounded themselves to provide a sense of purpose and security, and begin to see that what matters has been staring us in the face all along, if only we had had the eyes to see. We are then in a position to strip out what is no longer important to us and concentrate on what matters.

Such a perspective is at once both less complex than the labyrinthine systems we find necessary to deal with even the simplest of tasks today, and infinitely more subtle and demanding. It is about developing that personal and robust stance in the face of an ever-shifting reality that will enable us to separate the significant from the ephemeral, what needs to be resolved from what can be safely left to take care of itself. We must still our need to interfere. It is an eternal balancing act between intervening and going with the flow, understanding that, on the one hand, to alter something affects everything else while, on the other, to do nothing may make change more difficult in the future. To know when to act and when to leave well alone is the sign of wisdom and it is a commodity in short supply in our frenetic world.

We must find our own balance point in the ongoing tensions inherent in a world of opposites and put that unique perspective in the service of the community. For each of us will have a different take on life and in that diversity lies strength. Truth is something that none of us can ever truly grasp, but together we are more likely to approach its foothills. When people sensitively and creatively explore their differences then all involved are likely to be altered in the process and the results to be more hardy and long-lasting.

The problems we face today are no longer characterised by our ability to understand and master the world out there (as they were in the nineteenth century, for example, when simple public health measures made life tolerable in cities). They can be summarised by the question 'how can we live securely and sustainably on this crowded planet?' which is about our relationships with one another and the way we make collective decisions. From this perspective, it should be clear that our preoccupation with the objective, physical universe is blinding us to the real issues, if not actually making them worse. We need a greater insight into interpersonal relations and, through that understanding, to radically overhaul our systems of decision-making and conflict resolution, all of which appear to on the point of collapse. We need to concentrate on the moral universe rather than the physical one.

We also need to understand why we habitually act the way we do, both as individuals and as collectivities, and that means probing the depths of our unconscious to discover and acknowledge the wellsprings of negativity and destructiveness that are a so much a feature of our nature. That agenda might be seen as the province of the psychologist or social scientist, but more than anything else it represents a personal journey that each and every one of us must make. It is no longer a question of standing back, observing others and creating a theory, it is about creatively engaging with ourselves in a quest to find out who we are.

Only when we are at peace with ourselves and those around us are we likely to find ourselves in a position to review and renew our relationship with the physical universe. Once we begin to relate to those around us on the basis of mutuality we will begin to understand just how interdependent we all are, and that blurring of boundaries will extend to every aspect of the world out there. When we realise that our own health depends on the health of those around us, we will understand that our collective health is reflected in the health of the natural world of which we are part. We will have rediscovered the interconnectedness of all things, and our physical and moral universes will once again be one. We will once again have become spiritual as well as physical beings.

That does not imply that we should turn our back on science. Observation (the detachment of the observer from the observer) is only one part of the scientific method. Experiment (the engaging with the observed in a controlled way) is also basic to the approach, as is the employment of systematic doubt (a sceptical approach to results). If we accept that exploring who we are and how we relate to one another is the new project, then we are implicitly assuming that we are the experiment; we are both the observer and the observed and, to achieve the kind of new synthesis that is a condition for understanding, we must treat the information we are receiving critically. We are, in effect, adopting the scientific agenda. The difference is that we are not explicitly seeking to build up a body of objective knowledge through a sequence of activity that can be endlessly replicated. Rather, we are each embarking on a voyage whose outcome we can only perceive dimly, if at all. It is a shared journey based on a faith that the future of our planet depends on our ability to find a new paradigm that puts moral and spiritual awareness above material comfort. We will be moving into an era of uncertainty.

The route is not entirely unmapped. What happens in counselling is to some extent a controlled experiment. It is not a "normal" transaction between individuals, but one that is set up specifically to create the conditions for insight and subsequent changes in perception and behaviour. Although the counsellor observes the person they are working with, they are also observing themselves, assessing their own feelings and using them to throw light on what is happening in the session. They are also engaging with the other in a direct, human way and research suggests that the quality of the relationship is one of the key determinants of outcome.

Several suggestive themes are evident in this approach. First, counselling is definitely an outcome-based activity; lasting change is not only possible, it is the objective (primarily, but not exclusively, in the person attending counselling). Second, such change is most likely to happen within the context of relationships where we feel both safe and valued. Third, the individuals involved in counselling are caught up in a kind of ongoing dance that weaves a path between the inner and outer worlds, between engagement and detachment and between reason and emotion. It is an inherently unpredictable process that mirrors the reality of the human condition in a way that the modern world largely denies in its attempts to make life safe and predictable. Finally, it is about participation and connection, with the implicit assumption that the richer and more diverse that commitment is, the more we are opening ourselves up to the possibilities of change.

To know the other does not mean to have a catalogue of their likes and dislikes, of their skills and interests or to know their life history; it comes from embracing them as full human beings and being in community with them. The paradox is that, the greater that sense of identity with the other, the more aware one becomes not only of them as a many layered, remarkable being but of one's own complexity and uniqueness. Barriers recede and possibilities expand. Love truly is a virtuous circle.

We are ignorant about ourselves and each other in ways that would have been unthinkable in other cultures and at other times. The major religions of the world put an emphasis on love and an identification with the other ("Do unto others ..."); and yet we have created an environment where love and peace cannot prosper and where their opposites hate and violence are given full rein. Love comes when we trust in our fundamental sameness and interrelatedness, hate when fear creates difference and artificially divides us one from another. The conditions for love to flourish are more likely to be present in a Human Scale than in a mass society.

The emphasis that all religions have put on love should suggest that they have valuable insights to offer. For that reason alone, our secular tendency to simply dismiss the major religions as superstitious throwbacks to some unenlightened era when people acted out of fear and ignorance must be considered unenlightened. If the nature of reality is paradoxical, based on the balancing of polar opposites, then there can be no black and white answers to the problems we face on a daily basis. Life, by its nature, is inherently mysterious. The success of traditional science in concentrating on one aspect of that complex reality doesn't alter that basic insight.

In fact most people, including scientists, acknowledge that there are questions to which no answers exist: for example, does life have purpose and what are the implications either way? Our individual lives should in some way reflect our beliefs on this matter (they can only be beliefs because there is, as yet, no way of resolving the question – even the neo-Darwinists' claim that evolution provides an explanation of the way life has developed that doesn't require the mediation of purpose does not prove that it *isn't* shaping the reality we are engaged with). For those who sense that life has purpose the challenge is to glimpse its nature and find a way to respond.

Institutional religion has undoubtedly contributed more than its fair share of misery to the human lot down the centuries – and continues to do so. But that is no reason to throw the baby out with the bath water. All that the conflict, persecution and suffering that typifies religious wars (both internal and external) demonstrates is that no one faith has a monopoly on truth – if it had it would long since have triumphed over the others. It follows that *individual* enlightenment is as likely to be found in one as another and personal preference and circumstance will determine which path is followed. Religion can be a cage, but it can also liberate the individual from captivity. Some things cannot be put into words, they can only be experienced, but that is not to deny their validity.

If we are to fundamentally change the way we think and act, we must embrace uncertainty. By starting with ourselves and looking with fresh eyes at what is important in our lives, we may once again catch sight of the wonder that is inherent in all things. Engaging with others on the same journey will reawaken the dormant sense of spirit that resides in all of us.

Putting It All Together

This brief overview of the six dimensions that together mark out the territory of the Human Scale hopefully shows that they provide no simple answers. The more you explore them the more subtle and complex they appear. This complexity becomes even greater when you realise that they do not exist in isolation but are inextricably interconnected one with another. It is not possible to conceive of a situation where one of them – consensus, for example – scores ten on a scale of one to ten, while the others languish between three and four. Consensus depends on relationships based on mutuality, an acceptance of uncertainty and the presence of love in the transaction. It also needs something significant over which to reach consensus on, and that is really possible only in relation to things of immediate importance to the people gathered together – which will inevitably revolve around issues relating to food, work, energy or exchange that have to be local if people are to exert any meaningful control over them; which, in turn, implies an identification with place.

The bad news, then, is that we can't just concentrate on one dimension. The good news, however, is that any progress we make on one is likely to influence all the others positively. The skill comes initially in choosing activities that will offer the maximum return.

As a basis for decision-making these six values offer a closer fit to the complexity of the real world than any of our existing one-dimensional, and frequently opposed systems. They also provide a yardstick against which to measure progress. However, as with all human constructs they do not provide a once-and-for-all answer. Sooner or later they will begin to become less effective in the face of changes that they have been instrumental in bringing about, and will be superseded by a more appropriate way of looking at the world. That is the nature of the human condition.

Ultimately, it is only through exploring these values consensually that principles important to a particular community can be established and come to inform the daily practice of everyone involved. This statement of intent becomes the covenant that acts as a reference point and rallying cry for all those committed to seeing their community prosper. That is how the individual electrons will become aligned and capable of producing the energy that will enable people to shift mountains if they are so minded.

But, just as we need others to confirm our identity and sense of worth, it will be unhealthy for communities to exist in isolation. That growth and development occurs through interaction is as true of communities as it is of individuals. Conversely, the lack of such stimulation can lead to stagnation, self-satisfaction and the habituation of harmful and questionable practices – which is one of the stereotypes of traditional communities cut off from the wider world.

Communities will have to come together to discuss issues of mutual interest (e.g. the siting and upkeep of shared systems of communication, sharing resources such as water, etc.) and to plan and maintain joint enterprises that cannot be achieved in isolation. Although the emphasis throughout has been on the very local, there are activities that are carried out appropriately on a larger scale. While health, educational and cultural services, for example, can and should be a very local responsibility, there will be exceptions that may require the co-operation of several communities, or may even be more regional in nature – for example, university-type provision, specialist medical facilities, or libraries, theatres, etc. The guiding principles underlying these initiatives should be that:-

- Only those things that cannot be adequately provided in a local context should be considered appropriate to be developed on a wider scale, and

- The six values should be implicit in all aspects of the planning and implementation of such projects.

In other words, any decision-making structures that exist above the local level should be informed by the same considerations as apply in the basic cell (the local community). We are seeking to construct an organic model that responds in an appropriate and timely fashion. Thus, such bodies should be based on relationships, should seek to establish themselves as communities (which have a past and a future) and take significant decisions consensually; they should do nothing to diminish the availability of local food, work, energy and exchange, and should retain an identification with place and be able to live with uncertainty.

We are talking about a series of representative bodies (gatherings) that are grounded in each local community and stretch to cover regional and ultimately global perspectives. If the principle that only those matters that cannot be dealt with appropriately by lower decision-making communities can be dealt with by those above applies, then the business should get progressively less the further up the chain one travels – until, at the global level, the main focus will be on issues such as responding to natural disasters. Remember that in an organic model the constituent parts are self-organising and self-repairing and, for consciousness to intervene, is usually a sign of ill-health somewhere in the system.

The need identified above for ongoing trade between communities around the world suggests that regional and global currencies will evolve to facilitate such exchange, and individuals and groups may be operating at several levels at any one time. Part of the function of the gatherings above the basic community level will be to ensure that the financial systems appropriate to their level are transparent and based on sound and fair credit. It is possible to envisage regions borrowing from one another to deal with specific problems such as providing safe drinking water to remote areas or a collapse in the functioning of a specific community. In this way, the basis for a just social order spanning the globe can be created and provide the confidence that will ensure communities can live at peace with one another.

Joint ventures between neighbouring communities might need collective financing, not to mention the assemblies that stretch right up to global level. Systems of tithes will have to be to developed to fund these activities but, to use a possibly outworn phrase, there should be no taxation without representation and setting and agreeing these tithes is likely to be a time consuming business. But, once again, if lasting decisions can be reached, it will be time well spent. If two individuals (acting for a street of, say, a hundred people) were representatives on a wider neighbourhood gathering, it is easy to see that, very quickly, quite large areas would be covered – a hundred delegates would represent 50 x 100 = 5000 people (at the next level it would be 50 x 5000 = 25000).

The key issue is representation. Ultimately, we are all individuals and can only represent ourselves, but through consensus and its ability to align people to the same vision, it is possible for the one to act on behalf of the many. The person a community chooses to represent them will reflect their confidence in the individual's ability to hold the collective viewpoint while remaining themselves. They will look for people who embody the truths contained in the six dimensions of the Human Scale and who live them in their daily lives because, in seeking to create another community (the decision-making community they are representing their community on), they will be exposed to a different set of relationships and perceptions that will, if they are willing to live with uncertainty, inevitably challenge their own (and their community's) position. That ability to have feet in more than one community becomes an ever greater challenge the more distant the decision-making body gets from its constituent communities; a burden mitigated to some extent by the corresponding reduction in scope and depth of the issues participants are likely to face. Being a representative will be a burden as much as an honour and not something to be shouldered lightly.

How these decision-making constituencies are made up will ultimately depend on the communities themselves, but they are likely to reflect different realities to our existing forms of governance. For a start they will emphasise the quality of every individual's involvement in the process rather than the quantity of votes cast. Decision-making will be based on consensus and an acceptance of uncertainty as a creative part of that process. Most importantly, perhaps, they will be based on an identification with place and the need to nurture and protect a particular piece of land.

The six dimensions of the Human Scale provide a comprehensive guide to the issues that we need to tackle if we are to stop and then reverse the headlong rush towards disaster. But they are only a starting point. First we have to explore what they mean for us and those around us. Then we have to act, taking a step at a time, and relating that experience back to the six dimensions, providing a feedback loop that will enable us not only to check the progress we are making, but also to appreciate both how they interact and how one insight leads to another in an ever deepening spiral of understanding.

We now have the building blocks with which to start the task of rebuilding the world. The only question is HOW we set about assembling them to ensure the best chance of success.

Size is critical. Too small and the group may not have the resources to meet the challenge, too big and there is the danger of incoherence. The answer is to have the best of both worlds, the adaptability of the small coupled to the strength of the large. We are talking about an organic, systems approach, which sees organs (communities) comprising individual cells (people), and bodies (local, regional and global gatherings) being made up of communities. For the moment, however, we must continue to focus on the small if we are to remain true to our bottom-up approach.

7

The HOW Question, or "What Can I Do?"

By now you will perhaps have an idea of why life today is alternately so frustrating (all the systems and things that never quite work properly) and deeply depressing (decisions taken by governments that you know will make things worse rather than better) and why you feel that there is so little you can do to change the situation. You will also have some sense of the direction we need to be heading in if we are to respond successfully to the challenges we face. So, how do we as individuals go about changing the world?

One of the more obvious conclusions that we can draw from the analysis thus far is that trying to change the existing system is a waste of time – it's on autopilot – and it doesn't matter how hard or how long you batter away at the levers of power, the situation is only going to get worse. There are really only two sensible responses to this realisation:-

- To opt out completely and try and create one's own bit of sanity somewhere remote from the madness that surrounds us, or

- To ignore the wider madness completely and concentrate on building alternative sources of governance, ones that start from where we are and build from the bottom up, empowering local people to find local solutions to local problems.

The first option may seem attractive until one understands that there really is no escape. From Pole to Pole, the grip of the global juggernaut is getting stronger by the day. The only realistic way forward is to start to create the alternative from within. In case that seems just too hard and scary a task, the following quotation might help, "given the right circumstances, from no more than dreams, determination, and the liberty to try, quite ordinary people consistently do extraordinary things"[1]. We are all being given the licence to be extraordinary.

We also need to remind ourselves that major shifts in perspective rarely happen in a planned or even conscious way, but are the result of many different influences and initiatives coming together under the general heading of an idea whose time has come. As we have seen, the Industrial Revolution in England and Scotland grew from within a society that saw no pressing reason for altering the way it went about things. A system based on land, wealth and privilege was not about to change itself, but a new and seemingly innocuous element had entered the equation: a general interest in observing natural effects through experimentation. Born out of the Enlightenment belief in Reason, the eighteenth century produced an insatiable desire to understand Nature and use that knowledge for the improvement of the human lot.

Although the approach was initially haphazard, a general embracing of the value system that came to be called the scientific method drove this revolution in thinking and acting forward. Groups formed up and down the country, sharing the results of experiments and ideas. They were often dilettante dabblers wanting to be at the cutting edge of intellectual fashion, but engineers and entrepreneurs such as Josiah Wedgwood, Matthew Boulton and James Watt (and countless others who didn't succeed so spectacularly) saw opportunities to put the new insights to practical purpose: in many instances they were driven more by a desire to see their inspiration bear fruit than to make money[2].

As the new methods of production and power generation gained ground, however, so the vision of what was possible broadened. It was essentially a mechanical world view that produced a supreme confidence that all problems could be solved by sound engineering. Factories, armies, bureaucracies and communication systems could and should run like clockwork, while the whole system would be regulated through the objective measure of money. We are still living with the consequences.

Today, there is a general perception that the system of democracy that Western civilisation has evolved over the past two hundred years is state of the art and, if only the rest of the world would adopt it, everything in the garden would be rosy. There is little incentive to change the basic framework. Beneath that complacency, however, is a growing interest in alternative forms of decision-making, from community building to local currencies, from communal ownership of renewable energy schemes to eco-villages. What these projects share in common is a local focus that reflects the interactions of real individuals. As yet, they lack the kind of coherent value base that the scientific method provided for the Industrial Revolution. The six Human Scale values are intended to fill that gap and provide a common sense of direction.

Starting the Journey

We now understand WHAT we want to achieve (Sustainability – see definition on pages 7-8) and WHY (the six values – see page 97) we want to achieve it. We are ready to address the question of HOW, in the light of the answers to those other two questions, we should set about the task.

We are all different, with a variety of personalities, skills, resources and opportunities. Where we each start our journey will thus be different and it might take us a while to find a milieu in which we feel comfortable and where we can make a contribution. The important thing is to understand that there are simple steps that we can all take to live more sustainably *today*, without having to change anything else about the way we live (some suggestions are given in Appendix 2 – 102 Things YOU Can Do Right Now). The first step is often the most difficult but, once in motion, moving on becomes more natural than stopping. In the process, we may come to understand more about the wider consequences of the decisions we take each day almost without thinking. Every new thing starts with someone doing something differently.

Using less energy, switching to renewable sources, recycling, composting garden waste, etc., important as they are to limiting the impact of global warming, will not be sufficient in themselves to help us find long-term solutions to the challenges we face. That will take nothing less than an alternative vision of what is possible and desirable. As we have seen, playing with ideas and experimenting are the prerequisites of change. Mistakes are part of the process and failure an ever-present option, but the charm of new possibilities sustains people and they are irreversibly changed in the process. Sharing what does and doesn't work openly with others helps clarify the issues and produces both concepts and a language that are robust enough the carry the ideas forward. The individual electrons are becoming magnetised. Eventually a Divine Right of Kings Moment arrives when the future comes into direct conflict with the past and there is no turning back.

The six values of the Human Scale provide a way of checking that we remain on course, and to test even simple decisions against the question, "is this taking us closer to, or further away from where we want to be?" When disagreements arise it will be helpful to step back and ask what insights the six values offer about the particular issue in dispute, as a way of diffusing the natural tendency towards polarisation and the shouting matches that inevitably result. To use them in these ways they need to be internalised so that they become part of our mental furniture: and that implies exploring their parameters to the full, preferably discussing them with others so that a deeper understanding of their implications and the often subtle way in which they interrelate can be achieved.

One way to begin that process is to explore what it is about the way things are at present that makes them *in*human. An exercise that has proved helpful in this context is to imagine yourself moving to a foreign city where you can't speak the language, and to ask yourself how you'd feel and what problems you might encounter. People usually start by saying that they'd feel unsure of themselves, hesitant and insecure. A lot of day-to-day life would be familiar – skyscrapers, shopping malls and cars are international – but might not offer clues as to what is expected in particular circumstances. What is the etiquette for crossing the road? Is jay walking encouraged or frowned upon? And what are the consequences if you get it wrong?

The whole question of the law and its nuances of interpretation is something intangible and, if you don't have someone to hold your hand, you may give offence or find yourself condemned for actions that you believed to be entirely innocent. Dealing with government and private agencies to buy or rent a house, register for work or find a doctor are all based on social constructs and, as such, have no material existence. Short of reading all the legislation, they can be absorbed only by living them. The same is true of the many and varied customs and habits of your new surroundings. Not surprisingly, people feel vulnerable in such circumstances and, while that sense of hazard may fade over time, it is always there in the background. You can never feel entirely at home.

That, in a nutshell, is the situation we all face all the time in a world that is constantly changing, and where rules and regulations are made at some distant point and with little or no reference to ourselves. It is all just too big and out of our control. We are on the outside and do not feel engaged. As a result, we can never truly be at home and, to compensate, we feed the gnawing emptiness that is at the centre of our lives. We spend, spend, spend and in the process we are literally destroying our home. To recognise that we need to regain control over our own lives so that we can focus on what is important is the first step towards achieving a new world order.

The Iona Community[3] based in Scotland expects its members to undertake a regular personal audit and to account for their way of living in terms of time, money and prayer. The results are shared with other members and changes in lifestyle are discussed that will bring that person's life more into balance with the aims of the community. That kind of conscious exploration of what we think we are doing and what we are doing in practice is an invaluable way of monitoring change.

Each of the six values focuses on a different aspect of the task we each face. The awareness that they are interrelated, and that taking positive action on one will impact on all the others, means that we can choose to concentrate on those areas that we feel most confident in, or that reflect our natural interests. For some that will be exploring the relationships around them and trying to understand the implications of mutuality; for others it will involve very practical steps to safeguard their local environment. The important thing is to start a process that will begin to tilt the balance back towards a future that is sustainable for us and for our children.

Relationships – Based on Mutuality

We are relating to one another all the time, but it is the quality of those interactions – and particularly their degree of mutuality – that is the issue. To illustrate the point, look at a typical day and ask yourself how open and honest you can be with the people you engage with; and then pose the same question from their perspective. Only if you can imagine each party feeling comfortable sharing themselves with the other – and being happy to receive that confidence – can the relationship be described as mutual.

Most of our daily intercourse fails the test because we are talking to complete strangers or individuals we only see in a very limited context. How would we respond if the lady on the supermarket checkout began telling us how poor the produce was, or the problems they were having back in the warehouse? Even if we were prepared to listen sympathetically, we have nothing to offer that might help resolve her dissatisfaction. Most of the time, however, we don't want to know; we are busy people and need to be getting on with our lives. We don't want to engage, it's not our problem. But, in a mutual relationship, the issues the other person in the transaction is facing at that moment are our concern because we are relating to them as complete human beings, not as cardboard cut-outs designed as part of a machine to provide the illusion that our needs are being met.

In most of our relationships today we are partial beings because that is the way our society copes with the complexity of organising millions of people. We have functions – office worker, shopkeeper, manager – which create expectations in both ourselves and others, and lead to confusion and resentment if they are not observed. Only in our closest relations do we begin to experience ourselves as rounded beings with varied and conflicting needs and, even there, the opportunities for growth – the chance to resolve contradictory bits of ourselves – are limited because we rarely tackle challenges together. To develop we need other people who are engaged in the same process and who we trust enough to offer us considered and careful insights into what we are doing.

Another problem that we have to overcome in the pursuit of mutuality is to accept that authority is not linked to position or role, but is rather a manifestation of personal qualities. For me to defer to someone's authority is not the same thing as accepting that they have authority over me. In the first instance, I am acknowledging that they have more knowledge, experience or skill than me in a particular instance – I have choice in the matter: there is also the possibility that, in other scenarios, *my* authority will be recognised.

In the second, I am consenting to the other person dictating to me to a greater or lesser extent, even in situations where I may have more expertise than them – an element of choice has been removed from me (in the case of dictatorship, completely!). Where authority is linked to position there is always the danger that, however hard the parties may strive towards mutuality, domination and subordination will become part of the transaction. It is, at the end of the day, easier to give and receive orders than to continually negotiate a mutually acceptable way forward. We are only human, which is why power corrupts and absolute power corrupts absolutely.

How then do we increase the amount and degree of mutuality in our relationships? There are many techniques available for helping groups come together specifically for the purpose of helping one another cope with the ups and downs of life – including meditation, guided fantasies, the use of story, being in the present, etc. The simple answer, however, is that mutuality becomes a possibility every time we link with others in the pursuit of shared goals. It doesn't really matter what the objectives are as long as there is a shared passion and some tangible outcome.

Anything from a book-reading club to planning a series of social events can provide a vehicle to explore the nature of the relationships within the group, providing that is on the agenda from the start. It takes time for people to become comfortable with one another and, for that reason, there needs to be continuity in terms of the frequency and duration of coming together, as well as a commitment to ongoing membership. It is then a question of using the opportunities provided by the shared task to review and discuss the group's functioning, focusing on what is going well as much as the problems that are being encountered. By sharing observations about each other's contributions in a sensitive and supportive way, members of the group have the opportunity to reflect on the way they are perceived. It is always important not to dwell solely on the negatives but to stress the positives in any situation.

As a natural part of this process people will begin to bring up issues that are important to them at a particular moment, but which may have no apparent bearing on the purpose of the group. In the normal way of conducting business, such interventions would be ruled out of court, but they are relevant in so far as they are preventing someone participating fully in the group's activities. It may be more important for the long-term success of the project to take time to deal with the issues being raised, providing they are not allowed to take over.

Of course, until we are skilled in these matters, there is always the possibility of the experience being destructive, of individuals being unable to cope with the insights offered or trying to project on to others their own inadequacies. That is a danger inherent in all change, and mistakes will undoubtedly be made and damage done. But, until we gain the strength and inner knowledge to accept mutuality as part of our everyday experience, we are only at the starting line of the journey we are all going to have to make if life on this planet is to be truly sustainable.

Communities – Based on Love and Personal Responsibility

People need a degree of organisation, both in their personal lives and, more importantly, in the way they relate to one another. That need will be reflected in how communities are structured and each will be different. Like so much that we take to be real and immutable, however, such arrangements are nothing more than human constructs and can be changed. It is sometimes hard to remember that the sole reason for the existence of any structure is the realisation of a dream or vision. Something needs to be achieved and people have to come together to achieve it. Any structures, policies and procedures that may be adopted are secondary and should always be subject to the simple test of whether they further the vision or detract from it. If the answer to that question is not unequivocally in the affirmative then the system can and must be changed.

All too often bureaucratic organisations limit, distort and dilute the dreams that inspired their founders and, in that sense, the need to expand that follows success can be seen as the kiss of death to the creativity and excitement that typify a venture's early days. The point at which an organisation takes over from the individuals who compose it is a moot point, but it is likely to be small – somewhere between twelve and one hundred and fifty people. One way of translating that insight into our current context, in which all the pressures are to grow and get bigger, is to suggest that, rather than expanding as business develops, new ventures should replicate themselves. Each cell would then operate autonomously while benefiting from the existence of a wider community of interest (see next page).

Once an organisation has become entrenched it is very difficult to reclaim. In the same way, the dead hand of the law frustrates the ability to do things differently. Much of company law, for example, relates to ownership, dating back to the Industrial Revolution and the balance between encouraging the investment needed to fuel it and the liability that might result from cutting corners or sharp practice. Today, we are stumbling towards a much wider definition of stake holding – including employees, customers, the local community and even the environment itself – but we have no model (legal or otherwise) of how such a broad church might be accommodated. It is time for a Divine Right of Kings Moment.

Communities can and should be self-organising. In that sense small is beautiful because it is above all size that strangles love and its ability to create the kind of identification one with another that balances freedom and equality in a creative and life-affirming way (see pages 98-100). It also restricts the ability of individuals to take personal responsibility for their lives because so much is decided for them elsewhere. We need to rediscover the ground rules for collaborating in small groups to achieve common goals over time.

How we set about doing that will once again depend on our circumstances and who we are. To the very few who are in positions to influence the shape and structure of large organisations is given the opportunity to redefine the nature of the task. Instead of looking at a traditional top-down structure, with activities being controlled and delegated by the centre, a first step would be to envisage a circle of self-organising cells co-operating to achieve a common, jointly agreed goal facilitated by the expertise and resources available at the hub. Power has moved from the centre to the periphery and, in the process, the creativity and energy that were tied up in overcoming the inherent inertia of the bureaucracy is released. That is an alternative, more life-affirming, model of dealing with success and the inevitable demand to expand.

If the cells around the periphery are capable of making, and can be trusted to make, decisions that will be in the wider community's best interests, that freedom will be reflected in the language used to describe common activities. The words 'accountability' and 'supervision', for example, might be replaced by 'responsibility' and 'mentoring' to reflect the mutuality implicit in the relationships.

In 1970, in response to the need for new systems of global exchange, Dee Hock was invited to found the company that became Visa[4]. To work, Hock realised that the kind of credit card he envisaged could not be the property of a single bank (it wouldn't have the reach required for it to be used everywhere, and competition from cards launched by other banks would confuse customers and retailers alike) so he set out to create something that all banks could sign up to. The result was a product (the Visa card) that most banks now use. Visa International is owned by its members (cells) who, while directly competing with one another to attract customers to their particular cards, co-operate to promote the concept. The power is with the periphery (the cells) and the hub is the servant of the periphery in the sense that the members agree what the priorities are and how much finance should be available to achieve them: the process is essentially consensual and change comes from the periphery not the centre. Dee Hock called such structures chaordic (the balance between chaos and order). If such a radical shift in perspective is possible in the highly competitive world of international banking it can happen anywhere!

Most of us are not able to influence how our places of work are structured, but we are all part of potential communities in terms of the places where we live and the associations of which we are part. Some of those are more vibrant and full of potential than others and we should concentrate our energies where they are most likely to be effective. In parts of America there are still township meetings where residents can come together to discuss local issues. Rural parish councils in England provide another opportunity to get the issue of developing vibrant local communities on the agenda. There are many practical steps that can be taken to connect people who are effectively strangers to one another. It is possible, for example, to envisage streets connected by internet-style notice boards and chat rooms where people can share issues of mutual interest and concern, and get to know one another. Regular neighbourhood social events or open meetings to discuss common problems (including the implications of living sustainably) are other ways to get the ball rolling.

Ultimately, however, a group of individuals who know one another do not constitute a community. For that to happen there needs to be a shared vision, a shared identity and some common goals to work to. That becomes the basis of the covenant (see page 103) between the members and it can be achieved only through consensus. Some people are naturally better at reaching consensus than others but, like any other skill, it is one that everyone can learn and become competent in. And the more you do it the easier it becomes.

Local Decision-Making – Based on Consensus

As suggested in the previous chapter (see page 106), the key to good decision-making lies in choosing the appropriate method – authoritarian, consultative, participative, consensual – for the issue at hand. Consensus, however, provides the bedrock of any communal endeavour and offers a framework within which the other ways of taking decisions can be most effectively deployed. Put simply, unless there is agreement on the general, there is unlikely to be harmony on the specific. It comes back to the magnet analogy. If the electrons are aligned and producing a strong social charge, the decisions that individuals and groups take on a daily basis are likely to support and reinforce the general view of what is important; the momentum will be maintained. Without that commitment to shared values, however, there is likely to be chaos and confusion, leading to anger and frustration as what is achieved here is undone there. That is a recipe for a community at war with itself.

Of course, a shared perception of what matters in life is not sufficient in itself. It can all too often support the interests of one group at the expense of others and be reflected in the single-minded defence of certain behaviours and a desire to exclude all but the pure. It becomes a straitjacket that allows neither individuals nor the community itself to respond to changing circumstances. By contrast, maintaining consensus is a constant challenge to the status quo and has to be worked at. Every point of view must be heard and accommodated – particularly those that are confused and hesitant, because it is precisely they who are likely to be grappling with contradictions not yet fully apparent in the prevalent mindset. For that reason the process takes time and it requires all the skills that relationships based on mutuality imply.

So, how do you start? Various organisations offer frameworks within which people can explore what it means to work towards consensus. Community Building, based on the writings of M. Scott Peck[5], provides an introduction to being 'in community', an experience of the profound identification possible between self and other that creates an environment in which people feel safe to explore themselves and the barriers that exist between them openly and honestly. Other approaches, more explicitly aimed at the decision-making process, include the Institute of Cultural Affairs[6] and the Scarman Trust[7]. These organisations have evolved techniques and resources that allow groups of people who have never met before to sit down with one another and evolve a common view of the issues that confront them.

Consensus is most potent, however, in groups that are relatively stable, and that poses a real problem in a society where work is the most common form of association in many people's lives. Businesses do not seek stability; indeed transience and change are increasingly pursued for their own sake as a sign of corporate health. A moment's thought, however, suggests that effective decision-making is an issue even in the adrenalin-soaked pursuit of profit. Less haste, more speed would be one consequence of pursuing consensus. Time invested in exploring and agreeing an organisation's purpose and values (the 'what' and 'why' questions) at all levels would be reflected in greater consistency of decision-making throughout. If that opportunity were genuinely open to all employees, an explicit acceptance that the structure and its ethos might change as a result of such inclusive involvement would be required: it might even result in priorities other than the pursuit of the bottom line. Whatever the outcome, the health of the operation would be immeasurably improved and more effective feedback loops would have been introduced into what are often closed systems.

There is an increasing recognition that work groups function better if they operate openly and have the responsibility to determine the best way to achieve given outcomes. Such an approach puts the emphasis on the individual and what they have to offer rather than on position, age or background. It can be threatening to people used to set ways of doing things and of following or giving orders, but it fulfils one of the basic requirements of consensual decision-making, that participants come as themselves rather than as occupiers of roles. That, in turn, is a prerequisite of being able to freely explore ourselves and others in the search for common ground.

It is at the local, community level that the need for consensual decision-making is most needed and where it is increasingly least available. Unless everyone in a given neighbourhood has a common view on how to tackle the challenge of living together *sustainably* and feels that they have a genuine stake in what is happening around them, progress is likely to be haphazard. People will assume it is someone else's responsibility to take the initiative and, as we have seen, government – whether at national, regional or local levels – is not geared to deliver the kind of coherent, detailed programmes that are going to be necessary if each locality is to have its unique matrix of strengths and challenges acknowledged and responded to.

In the face of this dearth of opportunity, what can the individual do? Ironically, as the cost of government-provided services escalates, the need for volunteer input increases. In many settings – from public parks to hospital catering, from local conservation initiatives to charity shops – local people are becoming involved with, and plugging gaps in, local services. That provides an opportunity to influence what is happening locally and a consensual approach that produces a clear set of common priorities is more likely to shape – and may eventually come to lead – the wider agenda locally.

It is also possible to start from scratch, forming local interest groups that might tackle anything from litter to local recycling initiatives, from accessing local food to negotiating local energy agreements[8]. Gaining Fair Trade status for your community is an example of how local people can actively influence what is happening in their neighbourhood. The important thing is to be inclusive from the start and agree what is being done and why consensually. Success breeds success and the more examples there are, the more natural it will seem for local people to want to tackle local issues and have a say in everything that concerns them.

Consensus as the basic building block of community is not a new concept, just one that we have lost in our enthusiasm for large-scale innovation. It is part of our race memory and as natural as scooping up water to wash your face. When we find it again we will recognise and want to nurture it. It will feel like coming home.

Local Food/Local Work/Local Exchange/Local Energy – Based on Creativity and Sustainability

There are myriad opportunities for making connections locally. Instead of automatically shopping at a supermarket – which is unlikely to be local in the sense that we are talking about and will stock products from around the world, many of which are available locally – it is worth making the effort to find out what is available on your own doorstep.

Most farmers no longer produce for local markets. They have become cogs in the huge agribusiness project that treats food as any other commodity and where competition forces prices down in an ongoing battle to protect profitability. That produces an inevitable trend towards ever bigger agricultural units and the application of ever more technological fixes (in the form of computer-driven projections, high-tech machinery and, of course, more and more fertilisers and pesticides). It is neither healthy nor sustainable.

To encourage local farmers to produce the food we want in ways that can continue into the future, we are going to have to recognise that it isn't just another commodity to get the best deal we can on. That means putting our normal and habitual consumerist hats to one side and really asking questions about where food comes from and how it is produced. Local greengrocers are a dying breed, pushed to extinction by market forces, and the few survivors should be supported unreservedly. Developing relationships with shop keepers can be a way to encourage them to source their (preferably organic) food locally.

Where local shops don't exist, buying from farmers' markets, farm shops and box schemes (local, organic produce that is delivered to a central point in a community and then distributed to individuals in boxes) are other ways in which the trends can be reversed – although even here it is worth checking where food has actually come from – you may be surprised! Other options include local people developing direct links with local farmers, encouraging local shops to access food from them or, if necessary, setting up your own distribution system (charity shops provide one model, where a lot of the work is done by volunteers, thus keeping down the costs). As suggested in the previous chapter, it is even possible to conceive of local people going to work on their linked farms at times when the farmer needs additional help – another way of keeping the cost of food down. Willing Workers On Organic Farms (WWOOFers) is an international organisation providing a kind of cultural exchange in which individuals work on organic farms in exchange for board and lodging, which provides a convivial way of learning organic farming skills. Allotments are seeing a resurgence of interest and offer real opportunities for producing and marketing good food.

The issue of animal husbandry is a complex one, but in sourcing local milk and meat it is clearly important to consider the conditions in which animals are kept. Supermarkets have created conditions in which livestock are abused in ways that, if applied to humans, would be considered crimes against humanity. Slaughtering is done on an industrial scale with little or no consideration to the dignity or suffering of the living beings that are processed. They are reduced to things and we do hurt to ourselves when we ignore what is happening. If we take the life of any creature we should do it with consideration and gratitude for the gift that we are being given.

The possibility of local people preparing batches of ready-cooked meals has already been raised (see page 116). Skills of all sorts are widely available within a community even if they are not often recognised. The issue is how to put people who want a particular service in touch with those who can provide it. A simple directory detailing the products and services that can be accessed in the local area, and that can be backed up by word-of-mouth recommendation, provides a simple starting point. Such community or social enterprise needs support and investment at key points if it is to grow and prosper, and networks of local "business angels" would help such developments.

There are countless opportunities for such local, social entrepreneurship. At present, for example, there are many low energy light bulbs that can only be accessed through the internet, which means small packages being transported up and down the country. Far more sustainable would be a network of local shops carrying sufficient stock for local need. Failing that one or more local people might take on this warehousing and distribution function in their own home. With the aid of the local directories already described they would quickly become a successful focal point in the community. The same approach could be adopted for green household products and it is possible to envisage local support groups being set up to help new parents access green nappies and exchange second-hand clothes and equipment.

The key element in all such initiatives, however, is to recognise that any transaction undertaken is an exchange and should be negotiated on the basis of mutuality. Used to walking into a huge store and just picking up what we want, it is a skill that we need to re-learn. Quite apart from strengthening relationships, it can have benefits in other ways, as discussion will help clarify what it is that we actually want (as opposed to what supermarkets, etc. make us think that we want).

Local work is also more responsive to individual needs and circumstances. Rather than a one-size-fits-all approach that inevitably leaves many feeling excluded or dissatisfied, it is possible to tailor products and services more flexibly. For example, recycling services provided by local councils do not reach everyone. There are places the large vehicles required to make the service cost effective can't access; in some houses there's just nowhere to put boxes or wheelie-bins; and some people with disabilities just can't carry or manoeuvre, let alone put anything in them.

Suppose you were given the job of organising a service from the perspective of a particular street. Ideally all the residents would meet together and agree a way forward consensually. But perhaps that stage hasn't been reached yet, so you decide to visit each house. Everyone would have a different slant – their slant – on the problem and, in the process of discussing the options, both your and their view of what is desirable and possible will change.

It may take a little while, but problems can be resolved. Individuals' ability and willingness to become involved will be as varied as their personal circumstances, but the wonderful thing about planning at the human scale is that the complexity that is real life can be accommodated. The options suddenly appear unlimited and reflect the fact that, at the local level, releasing energy and initiative leads to people trying different things and responding flexibly and organically to changing circumstances. Your work will be rewarding not just for achieving its goals but for the human contact that it has engendered. The whole community is stronger as a result and will have increased confidence in its ability to resolve the challenges it faces. By contrast, centrally imposed solutions are limited (risks are rarely taken because the consequences of failure are so much greater) and tend to be inflexible and mechanistic.

Being able to generate its own energy (see pages 118-119) is another way in which a community can feel able to stand on its own two feet. Installing your own solar hot water systems or photo-voltaic arrays can be expensive (although grants are available in many European countries). Co-operatives are being formed to bulk-buy the equipment and train local installers in an attempt to make renewable energy sources more generally available. Ultimately, however, forms of community generation offer the most realistic way of achieving local independence of supply. Community-owned schemes are increasingly common and are usually organised on a co-operative basis (which limits the amount that any one individual can invest and makes share ownership more generally available – the minimum investment can be as little as £100). Although they favour local investors, investment from the wider public is usually both necessary and welcomed. By developing a "community of interest" of people keen to support such initiatives they are more likely to get off the ground and, as the numbers of such ventures multiply, it will be possible to "swap" shares to ensure that the support for each one is as local as possible.

Having an infrastructure of locally sourced food, supported by networks of local work and locally produced energy really makes sense only in the context of a system of local exchange (see pages 120-122) that can emphasise the importance of mutuality. Friends and neighbours coming together to exchange time, resources and skills through a token scheme (like a baby-sitting circle) offer a simple starting point. More sophisticated systems, such as Time Banks, Time Dollars and LETS, are examples of real trade being conducted successfully outside the conventional financial systems; some distribute their own currency, others depend on a paper or electronic debiting and crediting system[9].

Joining a local scheme is easy, setting one up from scratch less so – although there are several organisations that can offer help and advice to new groups[10]. The system can be tailored to the group or locality's needs; a church, for example, could ask its members to tithe a fixed amount that could then be spent on all the tasks needed to keep a congregation running, including visiting the sick. Most viable schemes manage to involve local businesses on the basis that a proportion of the cost of their goods or services can be paid for in local currency, improving customer loyalty and increasing the circulation of the alternative money. The evidence from these experiments in alternative currencies already suggests that they benefit communities by having a multiplier effect on wealth creation as well as strengthening both individual and group relationships.

From a local point of view it makes sense to invest in your own community, thereby ensuring that services you want are available in the area (if something is worth investing in, someone will support it and, if they come from elsewhere, part of the benefit will go to *their* community). There are examples of local shops issuing loan stock to finance an expansion. To prevent any increase in the number of restaurants, building societies and estate agents that already crowd our shopping streets, local people could buy or rent shops that become vacant and provide services that the community needs (greengrocers, for example). Often shops change hands very quickly and once an amenity has gone it is unlikely to return. A regional or national Community Trust[11], funded initially by donations and legacies, would be one way in which properties could be purchased quickly, thus giving local people time to organise themselves, eventually buying back the site through a community share issue.

This combination of food, work, energy and exchange provides a positive and creative context within which the challenge of sustainability can be tackled at a practical, everyday level. People are in control of the various processes necessary for a comfortable existence and, by ensuring that the individual decisions they are constantly taking are mediated by the other Human Scale values, there are always sufficient feedback loops to ensure that dangers are spotted before they become ecological or environmental catastrophes.

Identification With Place – Based on Oneness with Nature

When you consider that nearly two-thirds of all journeys between one and two miles are made by car, it is clear that most people can have only a very hazy picture of their local area. Combine that with the observation that decisions concerning the well-being of the neighbourhood are likely to be taken some distance away (in town halls, even by central government) by people you don't know, and it is hardly surprising that we have so little sense of investment in any place. Our pursuit of individualism has reached the stage where our self-contained units of housing reflect the way we operate as individuals. What happens outside our four walls is someone else's problem. Except, of course, what we do impacts on others and vice versa. And if we won't, or can't, share the wider responsibility for nurturing the environment we jointly occupy with one another and with nature, who will?

The first thing we need to do, then, is to get to know our localities in an entirely different way. Start by trying to imagine it as common land, with different features and offering a range of opportunities and resources. Then walk slowly round the area that falls within a radius of a mile from where you live and just observe what exists. From your new perspective as a partner in the stewardship of your common home, try to get a feel for its uniqueness. Why are things laid out the way they are and how do they fit together? What range of housing is there – what age, type and forms of ownership? Are there public spaces, streams, rivers, watercourses? How 'green' is the habitat – what is the ratio of concrete and brick to open ground; how many trees are there, what varieties and ages; what forms of wildlife are apparent?

This superficial audit can be supplemented by learning something of your area's background, looking at maps from the past to see how it has changed and developed, and reading local histories. Are there any plans for future development? Can you get involved in those decisions in any way? Find out what services are available, where they come from and how they get to you. Who is responsible for providing them and who monitors and controls them? We take so much for granted. When we turn on the tap we expect water will come out, end of story, but the more you look into these issues the more complex the world becomes and the more you realise that your area is indissolubly tied to other places, some many miles away, whose inhabitants have little sense of how they are linked to you.

What local associations are there (civic societies, environmental groups, friends of local parks, etc.) having some responsibility for the well-being of the area? Are there any local amenities (parks, playing fields, swimming pools) that might benefit from local support? How about shops and service providers (pubs, restaurants) within walking distance; are they patronised by local people and, if not, might they be prepared to change what they are offering to satisfy local demand?

By now you will be building up a multi-layered picture that includes the natural, physical (including the human-made) and social environments. How does this new knowledge and embryonic sense of place make you feel? Are you connected to or distanced from it? Are you proud to be part of your corner of the world, or ashamed? What aspects do you feel could be improved? What amenities should be provided locally that aren't? The answers to any of these questions can provide the spur to action. Anything from simple litter collecting to care for a local landmark, from encouraging wilderness areas that attract insects and small mammals to persuading local councils to plant more trees, can be a first step to beginning to identify with your local environment, to becoming a part of it rather than a parasite on it.

Knowing your place implies a familiarity with it that allows you to notice changes that would be invisible to a stranger, indicators of growth and fruitfulness or warning signs of damage and decay. By walking its bounds an awareness is created that leads to a deeper understanding of the passing seasons and the processes that sustain life. It will no longer be possible to see your neighbourhood as a series of individual housing units, each separate and entire in itself. And with that appreciation will come a desire to treat it as a whole. Existing boundaries will be seen as barriers to the realisation of a locality's potential (a series of back gardens joined together might be seen as a single field, for example). The notion of common land also suggests the need for a review of our existing forms of land tenure.

Fundamentally, however, the land we occupy (whatever the patterns of 'ownership') is not ours to do with as we wish. It is proper that we should seek to meet our own needs as a species, but the Earth does not exist for our benefit alone; it is a system that has its own complex rhythms and meaning, features of life that we have become detached from and which we ignore at our peril. We are part of that rich tapestry, but only a part, and the relationship we have with the rest of creation will determine what our future on this small planet is to be. We are exhorted to be stewards, but that is imperialism by another name. It presupposes an "us" and "them", a natural hierarchy in which we implicitly know what is best and that treats the natural world as a series of objects to be managed. It is the ultimate consumerist fantasy with everything neatly labelled and packaged (even nature trails are signposted and we are told where to stand to see something of interest).

The world just isn't like that, it is an organic whole, an unimaginably complex series of interconnected processes that is constantly changing and in which everything is affected by everything else. Until and unless we embrace that aspect of reality and have the humility to see ourselves as bit players in a drama that is unfolding, rather than as the scriptwriters, we will continue to create further crises. Any creature that routinely fouls its environment will reap the consequences. We must look to Nature to guide our actions, rather than wish to impose our will upon it; our relationship should be one of mutuality, not of power. As Richard Mabey puts it in *Nature Cure*, "our biggest challenge as a species is to work out a common arena with nature, a hinterland where we can accept each other's company and live out a relationship somewhere between the ten-day wilderness experience and the short stroll along a fenced trail"[12].

The more we can identify with the ground of our being – literally the earth beneath our feet – the more likely it is that we will recognise its vulnerability, particularly to what we as human beings so casually do to it. A sustainable future depends on our ability to nurture and protect our place for the long term.

Living With Uncertainty – Based on Spirituality

We like our lives to be predictable both as individuals and as a society. Although life is inherently unsafe and inscrutable, we rationalise the dangers in terms of risk statistics and seek to apportion blame when things do go wrong. It is a materialist, detached approach to reality. Institutional religion fulfills the same function, equating a virtuous life in the face of adversity with being saved in the hereafter. Neither approach acknowledges uncertainty. On the one hand science defines what its method can't explain as being unscientific and akin to superstition; on the other religion demands faith in doctrine that has been handed down over the centuries and interpreted by the establishment hierarchy.

It is natural to want simple explanations. Bombarded with information from every direction we have to simplify to survive. If we pondered every twist and turn of existence we would end up doing nothing. But that is very different from turning one's back on the possibility that the assumptions we operate on may be faulty or even wrong. Many of the theoretical advances in science are said to be counter-intuitive, but that simply means they run counter to our established way of looking at things. To turn a tap clockwise to get water is counter-intuitive because we are so used to turning it the other way: that's the way taps work in our world – but we could get used to the opposite convention and, in time, it would seem equally natural.

We are so used to a world in which laws, contracts, timetables and ways of working determine how we live our lives that it takes a moment to realise that they are human constructs relevant only in so far as they satisfy human needs and fulfil some vision about what is important. When we further observe that, not only do many of these social structures date back to times when the problems that confront us today were non-existent, but that they actually form the straitjacket that is preventing us from addressing those issues, we are facing a Divine Right of Kings Moment. We either carry on with a system that we know is causing an ever-worsening crisis, or we do something about it. We have to think the unthinkable and act on the conclusions we reach, even if that means turning our backs on all that has hitherto seemed natural and right.

To try and work out what is truly important in our lives means going beyond our habitual comfort zone and experiencing uncertainty. It is symptomatic of our age that people resort to extreme sports to confront themselves and come to terms with who they are. Certainly we need to understand ourselves better but, in changing the ways we think and act, we are more likely to need the stimulus of other people engaged in the same process than the adrenalin rush induced by embracing physical danger. If we are to live securely and sustainably on this crowded planet we must reach out and try to understand the other. We each have our own version of the truth and to explore its validity means having the humility and openness to hear and acknowledge where someone else is coming from.

In the eighteenth century, as we have seen, meetings were held up and down the country where people discussed the latest scientific developments and tested them out for themselves. Where questions remained, they devised experiments in the hope that they might supply the missing information or insight. It was the age of the amateur; there was tremendous enthusiasm and optimism across the whole range of scientific endeavour, and a generation became scientifically literate almost overnight. It was the beginning of the rigorous exploration of our physical universe that we take for granted today.

Something similar needs to happen in relation to the challenge of changing the ways we think and act towards one another (our moral universe, with sustainability as a key theme). Groups might come together for specific and quite practical purposes – recycling, alternative currencies, local food, conservation, etc. – but come to recognise that all these issues are interrelated and have to do with individual lifestyles as much as government policy. Discussion might then move on to looking at the obstacles to individual change and the assumptions on which we all act. Mechanisms for disseminating information to and between such groups would develop and provide a further impetus towards open and honest exchange. The internet provides an obvious vehicle for such developments.

We need to experience the potential of community building to create the circumstances in which love can flourish. Again, that means taking risks and facing the possibility of failure or rejection. Profound religious understanding can take a lifetime of self-discipline and faith but, if the desire to explore one's spiritual nature supports the belief that life has purpose requiring the active involvement of each and every one of us in its realisation, then we surely owe it to ourselves to take some tentative steps in that direction. Faith communities are obvious places to think and act in relation to the issues raised in this book. Membership is no guarantee of righteousness, but it can be an important part of a journey towards self-discovery. Such fellowships can exist both in and outside established Churches, but the rapid increase in both the number of sects and the fundamentalist nature of some of them, is a hazard for the impressionable, and care should be taken in selecting where to commit time and energy.

We need to re-engage with the natural world in a way that acknowledges our interdependence with it. Identification with place will help in that process, but it is also part of approaching the other in all its guises with dignity and respect, and having a reverence for all living beings. It is about engaging with, rather than detaching oneself from, life and sensing the mystery and majesty that lies at the heart of nature.

Ultimately, however, the exploration of a social order based on the Human Scale will reawaken both an ever expanding sense of wonder at the world we share with creation and an increasing sense of identification one with another. That in itself will foster a willingness to live in the moment and to tailor our understanding to the ever-shifting realities that confront us. We will have become comfortable living with uncertainty.

Conclusion

Take a moment to reflect on your feelings as you reach the end of this book. Hopefully, you will have a sense of the distance that has been travelled from a world that seems out of control and heading for disaster, to one where an acceptance of uncertainty actually brings a sense of peace; through knowing what we can do and what we must let be, trusting in the ordering of nature of which we a part. That is a measure of the distance that we as a culture will have to cover if we are to heal our damaged social fabric and nurture the environment on which we all depend.

The six Human Scale values provide a formidable agenda. Together they mark out the territory we are going to have to occupy if we are to create the systems of governance that will enable us to step back from the abyss that current forms of decision-making have brought us to. The task is nothing less than a complete re-think of the moral universe we share with one another. Only by exploring and understanding the nature and quality of the relationships around us are we likely to find a way to live securely and harmoniously on this crowded planet. Hopefully, this brief overview of some of the options available will have provided ideas about next steps that can be taken. They are far from exhaustive and one of the exciting aspects of doing things differently is that new ways of thinking and acting can appear as if from nowhere. We must be prepared to be surprised.

Whatever tomorrow holds, however, it will be civil society that determines its course. That swirling mix of families, friends, volunteers, local organisations and associations, churches, interest groups and chance meetings with strangers provides the melting pot within which the future will be invented and tested to destruction. As Margaret Mead put it, "never doubt that a small group of thoughtful, committed citizens can change to world: indeed it is the only thing that ever has"[13].

Postscript

Life on Earth faces arguably its greatest threat since the extinction of the dinosaurs. And it comes, not from outer space, but from the species that should be most aware of what it is doing – us. If we continue as we are at present we face a series of ever-worsening crises that will lead to the disintegration and destruction of whole species, ecosystems and human cultures – it may even lead to the demise of life itself.

We have to live to learn to live sustainably and that means making fundamental changes in the way we think and act as individuals and as communities, on a local, regional and global basis. Only by addressing the moral (as opposed to the physical) universe we all inhabit can we hope to find the way forward. The central question is whether Western concepts of freedom and democracy can be adapted to meet that challenge, or whether they are irredeemably part of the problem. Certainly, the far-reaching issues we face are the direct consequence of the way Western civilisation has sought to impose its vision of what constitutes the good life (which includes notions of freedom and democracy) on the world. In rejecting the materialist package, many turn their backs on a political system that they see as being inherently unjust if not imperialist in nature. When looked at from a Human Scale perspective, however, these ideas take on a fresh resonance and offer the possibility of humankind living securely and sustainably on this crowded planet.

The bad news is that we cannot look to a visionary leader or revolutionary scientific breakthrough to wave a magic wand and make everything continue more or less as it is. It is down to each and every one of us to begin to make the changes that are necessary if our children's children are to enjoy any quality of life. Some will act more quickly than others and begin to show the way, but there can be no lagging behind, hoping against hope for a quiet life or a last-minute reprieve from responsibility.

The good news is that we all are free, as yet, to stand outside the way of thinking that is leading us inexorably towards catastrophe. We can act differently if we choose. The first step is the hardest, but it will suggest the next and so on. By acting with others we are more likely to ensure that what we are doing is both appropriate and lasting. Making decisions is fundamental to the human condition and it is only by changing both the choices we make and how we take them, that long term change occurs. If we apply the vision encapsulated in the six Human Scale values to everything we do, the resulting decisions will become increasingly coherent and aligned. The social magnet will become charged and produce the kind of power that can literally move mountains.

Working to create a sustainable future for ourselves and future generations may just be the issue that unites our fractured and fractious planet. When that happens a Divine Right of Kings Moment will have truly occurred.

It is time to wake up and act.

Appendix 1
The Challenges Outlined

Global Warming and Unpredictable Climate Change

There is now a virtual consensus amongst scientists (even in America, where resistance to the idea has been greatest) that global warming is a reality. It is not a question of "if" but "when", "by how much" and "with what impact". Sophisticated computer programmes run possible scenarios and come up with predictions that America will suffer both severe droughts and flooding, along with searing temperatures in urban areas. The same is true of southern England where a return of vineyards and a weakening of the Gulf Stream that warms Western Europe, creating a climate in London and the Home Counties more akin to Labrador, are both being forecast.

What is clear is that rising sea levels will threaten whole peoples, predominantly in poorer parts of the world (although large parts of Florida could be completely submerged and nearly two million homes in Britain risk flooding, along with three-fifths of the country's best farmland[1]). Islands across the globe are in danger of disappearing beneath the waves and huge areas in low-lying coastal areas such as Bangladesh and the Nile Delta are threatened, potentially driving hundreds of millions of people from their homes.

And in the background is an apocalyptic vision of an uncontrollable chain reaction triggered by the release of carbon dioxide currently locked in the rainforests of the Amazon Basin. From being a net absorber of carbon – a carbon sink – they could become net emitters. If that were to happen global temperatures would leap. Recent rises in temperature may appear to be gradual and incremental but, as in all dynamic systems, there comes a point when the steady state 'flips' into something entirely different; and the suggestion is that that 'something different' will be runaway temperature rise coupled with a fundamental change in the regulatory systems that govern the world's climate.

Worse still, vast amounts of an even more vicious greenhouse gas, methane (with sixty times the impact of carbon dioxide), exists in the world's oceans. The result of the natural decay of organic matter, it is held in a semi-solid form by pressure and low temperatures. If the seas warm up as a result of global warming caused by carbon dioxide, the results could be catastrophic.

No one knows whether these doomsday scenarios could happen in reality or, if they did, where the threshold would lie and what the consequences might be, but the precautionary principle suggests that we should not be taking the chance. When the Chief Scientist to the UK government says that global warming poses a greater threat to the planet than terrorism, it is time to listen[2] ...

At the very least, future generations will have to contend with unpredictable periods of severe weather, dwarfing existing hurricanes and tornados in both frequency and force.

Resource Depletion (especially oil) and Environmental Degradation

In common with all civilisations we depend on energy and raw materials. In the years since the Second World War there has been an escalating scramble to rip natural resources from the Earth, leaving a trail of ecological and environmental damage in its wake. As the easiest sources of extraction have been exhausted, the despoliation has become worse as whole areas are laid waste. Recent flooding in the Philippines has been linked directly to (mainly illegal) logging.

We are hardly aware of what we are doing. Our bodies build up harmful substances (we in the West have up to a thousand times more lead in our tissue than is good for us and hazardous chemicals are now found in the bodies of *all* new-born babies), our agri-business methods of farming leave the land effectively sterile and in need of ever more injections of fertiliser and pesticides, our industrial practices pollute and diminish our supplies of clean water (natural water tables across America and Europe are being overused to the point where they may disappear altogether) and we continue to plunder metals and other chemicals as if we lived in a supermarket whose shelves were endlessly replenished. And, as we have seen with climate change, environmental collapse is not the consequence of a slow build-up of abuse, with ever clearer signs that some boundary is about to be crossed. It can happen like the flick of a switch: one second the light is burning, the next it is extinguished – in the case of particular areas of the world, perhaps for ever.

The destruction we cause is even not always visible. Fish stocks in the North Sea have been diminishing for decades and have now reached the point where there is a risk of it becoming a lifeless sea. As well as its being among the busiest shipping lanes in the world (around 400,000 tonnes of crude oil is accidentally spilled by supertankers – equivalent to four running aground – every year[4]), modern fishing vessels dredge and churn up the seabed in pursuit of a diminishing catch (plaice caught today are a quarter of the size of those a hundred years ago, cod are 60% smaller)[5], upsetting delicate ecosystems. The same is happening in the Atlantic and it is estimated that as many as ten thousand dolphins and porpoises are killed each year as "by-catch". Some whales have absorbed so much pollution that they would be considered toxic waste if they were on dry land[6].

Most worrying in terms of the continuance of Western civilisation is the situation regarding oil. Some analysts predict that "peak oil" – the point at which production peaks before beginning an inevitable decline no matter what the demand – is already upon us, most that it may be ten years away at best, yet others that it will be thirty years before shortages really begin to bite. Perhaps significantly, it is over twenty-five years since the discovery of new oil reserves exceeded consumption and around 50% of the most important oil producing nations (like the US and UK) are past their peaks and production is declining. We may not be out of oil yet but we are running on empty. Meanwhile, demand is continuing to increase, fuelled by near double figure growth in China and India. Oil prices will inevitably rise and, when we reach the point at which supply can no longer meet demand, we'll be fighting over the stuff. Many believe that point has already been reached.

Again, it's not a question of "if" but "when"'. Considering that 99% of our food depends on oil in some form or another and a third of all the energy we consume is expended on transportation (driven by the internal combustion engine for which there is no obvious alternative), it is not hard to foresee the impact on our lifestyles of a permanent shortfall in supply. For two weeks in 2000, truckers in the UK blockaded petrol tankers in their terminals. Limited supplies continued to reach the pumps, but nevertheless there was panic buying, with incidents of people fighting over bread in supermarkets. MI5, the British security service responsible for internal security, works on the basis that, in the event of such disruptions, the nation is only four meals away from anarchy[7].

The oil industry is bullish, confident that ways will always be found to meet demand. As oil prices rise, technology that is currently uneconomic suddenly begins to look attractive. Oil shale and tar sands are touted as potential sources, but the impact on the environment of extracting the oil will be disastrous. From an energy point of view they don't make much sense either: for each unit of energy used in the process you only get one and a half units of oil energy back – with conventional oil you get thirty times.

At the very least, future generations will have to contend with significant disruption to supplies of essential foodstuffs and other necessary resources.

Species Extinction and a Reduction in Bio-diversity

Mass extinctions are believed to have happened five times in the earth's history, triggered by cataclysmic events such as the asteroid strike in the Gulf of Mexico that, it is suggested, wiped out the dinosaurs. Extinctions are going on all the time and represent a natural part of the evolving system that is life. New variations of existing species are continually coming into being and old ones are marginalised and die out. In the geological timescale, in fact, the Earth has never been more diverse. Until recently. We are now experiencing a rate of extinction estimated to be a thousand times greater than would occur naturally (a rate greater than at the time of any of the previous mass extinctions). The increase is almost entirely the result of human activity and our relentless pursuit of food, water and natural resources, and will be accelerated further by global warming. Habitat loss (and fragmentation through road building, crop planting), over-exploitation through fishing etc., pollution and the introduction of non-native species are all contributing to what is rapidly becoming a crisis situation.

The process is going on all around us. It has been estimated that some 50% of the world's flora and fauna are in danger of extinction within a hundred years, including a quarter of all mammals, one in every eight birds and one in every three amphibians[3]. Indonesia, India, Brazil and China are among the nations whose animal and bird life is most under threat, while plant species are declining most rapidly in South and Central America, Central and West Africa and South East Asia. The warming of the oceans is already causing corals worldwide to die and, in areas such as the Seychelles, is killing extensive areas of plankton – close to the bottom of the marine food chain – leading to algae flushes that effectively suffocate marine life.

Bio-diversity matters at both a local and a global level because the higher mammals (including humankind) depend on healthy and complex ecosystems to survive. Put simply, if species lower down the food chain are not able to feed and reproduce successfully there is less to go round for the predators at the top of the tree and fewer can be supported. The richer and more complex the systems, the more robust they are when changes (such as global warming) occur. The Gaia theory propounded by James Lovelock portrays life as a self-regulatory, organic system; the well-being of the whole depends on the well-being of the parts. If the very fabric of nature is damaged by the removal of a significant number of its individual fibres, the resilience of the whole is weakened.

At the very least, future generations will have to contend with a world that is monochrome by comparison with today, reflected in a much reduced variety of plants and animals.

Population Pressure and the Resulting Rise in Disease and Food/Water Shortages

No one knows what the carrying capacity of the Earth is in terms of human beings because the impact of our current way of living is out of all proportion to our actual presence on the planet (we represent only 0.014% of the planet's biomass and 0.44% of the biomass of all animals[8]. The world's population continues to increase (although not at the rate that was predicted some years ago) and the UN estimates it will reach 8.9 billion by 2050. The pressures on land use, on access to clean and on sufficient drinking water, and sources of energy will continue to grow, particularly as areas such as China and the Indian subcontinent flex their economic muscle; the result will be increased deforestation, environmental degradation and consumption of irreplaceable natural resources.

The impact on people will be no less catastrophic. Already one in six people on the planet suffer from hunger and malnutrition and it is estimated that two-thirds of the world's population will be living in areas of acute water stress by 2025[9]. Cities will mushroom. By 2010 some 51% of us will live in cities with populations of a million plus (implying an additional three hundred growing from smaller, existing urban areas)[10]. The rapid urbanisation that characterised the Industrial Revolution produced conditions so dire that disease was endemic. The industrial processes themselves were unsafe and unhealthy, and produced working conditions that were little better than slavery. We face similar but much greater challenges if we are to find effective ways of coping with the predicted expansion either locally or globally.

The shantytowns that are a blight on so many cities in the euphemistically termed developing world are a visible manifestation of the problems, but they conceal a web of degradation and exploitation that stretches across the globe and implicates us all. They are also a breeding ground for disease that, with the ceaseless movement of people by air and sea, is easily transmitted from continent to continent. Near-ideal conditions for genetic mutation prevail and it is only a matter of time before we face a pandemic on the scale of the flu outbreak in 1919 or even the Black Death.

At the very least, future generations will have to contend with continuing and worsening images of poverty and periodic pandemic health scares.

The Impact of War and Terrorism

Since the end of the Second World War there has been no let-up in conflict across the globe – in fact, if movements such as the Basque Separatists are included, the incidence has been increasing in terms of the number of different locations where hostilities are taking place at any one time. Genocide, torture and terror are now the order of the day and we barely notice. Children are caught up in school sieges in Russia, prisoners are mistreated in Iraq, bombs explode anywhere and bring the predictable outpouring of grief and recrimination in their wake. The world is a less safe place.

9/11 changed many things, but one of its less obvious consequences was a general decline in trust. Doubt has been sown and, however momentarily, we now approach strangers, especially those with a different skin colour, more warily. Our external world may show small signs of this increased vigilance, but it is within that the change has been most profound. Our social fabric depends on trust, on the assumption that other people are generally like us and will approach life with goodwill and good intention. It's what makes collective action beyond the immediate bounds of friends and family possible, creating a social glue that binds us together. Once that sense of common identity goes, feelings of isolation and threat set in, further eroding the will to connect and making negative images of those who are different to us that much easier to sustain. It also accentuates and draws attention to the differences between the rich and the poor, the successful and the less successful and all the other weaknesses in the social fabric, fuelling a sense of grievance and envy. The world may have become a less safe place but, in our perception, it has become a dangerous one.

In these circumstances, it is more difficult to create the kind of environment in which peoples can come together to explore and resolve mutual difficulties and that, in itself, provides the potential spark for further conflict. And so it goes on; something that might once have been relatively simple to work out becomes buried under an avalanche of accusation and counter-accusation, of real or imagined wrong, until neither side has the energy nor will to do anything other than continue to slug it out. One only has to look at intractable hotspots like the Middle East to get a glimpse of the way the world is heading generally. And with competition for land, water, oil and other resources exacerbated by diminishing reserves and continuing population growth, it will be sooner rather than later.

At the very least, future generations will have to contend with a less secure world in which random acts of violence and images of untold misery become commonplace.

Appendix 2
102 Things YOU Can Do Right Now

It has been said that doing just three things would save the planet -

1) Stop shopping at supermarkets

2) Stop shopping at supermarkets

3) Stop shopping at supermarkets

While there is an element of truth in this statement, it would be unfair to totally demonise supermarkets. They do what they do only because we choose to let them. And therein lies the clue to beginning to live more sustainably. We have to choose to do it. As we have seen, changing behaviour is hard; we all have in-built resistances. The following suggestions are all simple and they can be achieved today (or the next day). They aren't exhaustive, but seeing the range and variety may help to get you started.

You can't change everything at once. That's what puts a lot of people off from even taking the first. Much better to start with something you feel confident you CAN achieve. Nothing breeds success like success and, once you have made that first step, the next will likely suggest itself and, before you know it, a lot of things will have changed for the better.

Remember the three Rs – Reduce, Reuse, Recycle. Recycling is good, but much more expensive than reusing and reducing. Reuse is better, reduce is best of all!

Food and Preparing Food

Use your "LOAF" – Local, Organic, Animal Friendly, Fair Trade

1. Make a point of buying produce that sourced locally, is organic and/or Fair Trade produce (organic food, particularly, uses less energy to grow, Fair Trade helps farmers elsewhere look after their environment – we're all part of the same world). However, it is worth bearing in mind that 95% of fruit and 50% of vegetables in Britain are imported[1], so choose carefully to avoid the energy costs of food miles (every calorie you get from a carrot flown in from South Africa has 'cost' 68 calories in fuel to be grown and get to you[2]). Ask where things come from and how they got to the shop. Questions and feedback are what makes shopkeepers change

2. Get into the routine of shopping daily in local shops for vegetables and meat, rather than doing a week's shopping, which inevitably requires a car no matter how close the shops are. The food will be fresher and you'll throw less away (see below). You'll also help reverse the trend of local shops closing – 8600 independent grocery stores (25% of the total) closed between 2000 and 2005[3]. Adopt a "one-shop" policy by avoiding chains. It has been estimated that each pound spent locally is worth £1.76 to the local economy, but only £0.36 if spent outside the area[4].

3. Buy food that is in season. It's more likely to be produced locally and it will help re-establish a connection with the natural rhythms of life.

4. Think holistically about the food you buy – how was it produced, where has it come from, what networks were required to sustain its production. It all helps to sensitise

yourself to the fact that everything we buy has a history. Knowing that history puts you in a better position to decide how sustainable the practices are. If you don't know the answer to these questions, ask the shopkeeper. That may get someone else thinking about the issues.

5 Bulk buy items that can be stored – organic oats, rice – as this saves on journeys and packaging. Better still, get it delivered.

6 Find out where your nearest farm shop, farmers' market and/or local box schemes are

7 Put the information you gather together and create a local guide or to good, local food outlets to distribute locally. Gradually increase its scope to include all ethical, sustainable shopping.

8 Avoid using plastic bags. Patronise shops that offer you paper bags or invest in a "Bag for Life" – i.e. one that is made from (Fair Trade) organic materials and can be used time and time again. Buy products with less packaging (up to a quarter of the rubbish we throw away is packaging)[5].

9 Use a steamer for vegetables – you need to heat less water – and put lids on pans. Match the size of the saucepan to the size of the ring. In general, don't use more water than you need for boiling vegetables, pasta and rice. Chop meat and vegetables into smaller pieces to reduce cooking time.

10 Plan your cooking so that the whole oven is used (30 minutes at 200°C uses 0.9kWh in an electric fan oven – cooking four things at the same time thus saves 2.7 kWh[6]). Batch cook.

11 Use a slow cooker and save 10-50% of the energy required to cook a meal (another advantage is that food doesn't burn if it's left!). It's ideal for single people. A hay Box works in a similar way – just heat up your food conventionally and then place it in the hay Box to finish cooking under its own heat.

12 Use a microwave for small meals.

13 Grow your own vegetables. It'll put you back in touch with the seasons, cost you very little and taste great! If you don't have a garden, find an allotment.

14 Don't use pesticides on your garden.

15 Eat less meat. Buy free-range produce.

16 Bake your own bread. Anything homemade helps reduce food miles and waste from packaging.

17 Cook for one another.

18 Eat in local restaurants and cafés that source local, organic and/or Fair Trade produce.

19 Learn how to make jams and chutneys; they taste better than the bought stuff and you know exactly what went into them. Preserve vegetables and meat – freezing is an excellent method, but it only takes one power cut to ruin everything.

20 Only fill your kettle with the amount of water you're actually going to use. Boiling one half full instead of full once a day could save enough electricity for an hour of television[7].

21 Keep fridge doors closed – for every minute the door is open it takes three minutes for it to regain its temperature[8]. Always allow food to cool to room temperature before putting it in the fridge.

22 If you don't have a freezer that defrosts automatically, defrost it regularly to prevent ice build up and increased energy inefficiency.

23 Avoid using a dishwasher. If you have to, set it for the lowest practicable temperature. Remember energy is used to clean and deliver water to your home.

24 Encourage children to drink water from the tap rather than always buying another plastic bottle. Use the same bottle and re-fill it!

Clothes and Fashion

25 Make your own clothes.

26 Fix something instead of buying new. Sewing on a button can give you a sense of achievement!

27 Buy second-hand or recycled clothing.

28 Ask yourself why you're buying new clothing: do you really need it or are you indulging in shopping therapy?

29 If your wardrobe is full of clothes you'll never wear again, bag them up and take them to your local charity shop or clothing bank.

30 As children grow out of clothes, pass them on to younger children.

31 Buy clothes made from natural materials, e.g. organic cotton.

32 Buy clothes made by ethical trading companies.

33 Use washing machines with a full load and on low-temperature programmes (choosing a 40°C washing cycle rather than 60° saves a third on electricity[9]). If you have to use a dryer, spin-dry wet clothes first. Remember to turn off at the mains after use.

Getting Around

34 Walk or cycle whenever possible. It's healthier, better for the environment and you learn more about your neighbourhood than you ever would behind the wheel of a car. Most car journeys are under five miles. By doing just one regular journey of one or two miles on foot you'll be significantly cutting carbon dioxide emissions.

35 Use public transport. It can take longer and may not be so convenient, but it's really just a question of planning your day better. Less haste, more speed!

36 Share a car or join a car-sharing club

37 Don't buy a new car (around 20% of the energy consumed over the car's complete lifecycle go into its manufacture[10]) and, if you do, try not to change it so often

38 If you do buy a new car, choose one that is smaller than your last one and that can be powered by greener fuels, e.g. bio-diesel, ethanol, lpg, etc.

39 If you have a car, drive well, save energy! Driving technique can improve consumption by up to 40% in urban areas or 22% on motorways[11]. Anticipate traffic situations with calm driving by looking, and think ahead. Drive at the lowest rpm. in the highest gear consistent with the conditions. Use the vehicle's momentum to drive smoothly. Use auxiliary equipment – like air conditioning – selectively. Switch off the engine when it is safe to do so. Remove unnecessary cargo from the car to reduce weight. Reduce aerodynamic drag whenever possible by removing roof and other racks when not in use and keeping sun roofs closed.

40 Check and adjust tyre pressures regularly, Properly inflated tyres can increase fuel consumption by up to 10%[12].

41 Lessen the social and environmental impact of your holidays by choosing an "Eco Holiday".

42 Offset the Carbon Dioxide emissions of your travel – including flying. Several internet sites (e.g. www.carbonneutral.com) calculate the green house gases generated by your journey and tell you how much you have to contribute to community projects to neutralise them.

Saving Energy

43 Get an energy audit done on your house or workplace, it could save you thousands. Keep an energy log of your consumption (don't forget your car and other travel!) and monitor your peaks. Try to work out why they are being caused and take action to reduce them. Set yourself targets for reducing your use of energy

44 Switch off – £47million worth of energy is wasted by mobile phone chargers alone; don't leave appliances on stand-by as this wastes another £744million worth. Up to 85% of power used by a VCR is consumed when on standby: appliances on standby pump one million tonnes of carbon into the atmosphere[13].

45 Insulate, insulate, insulate: insulating your loft to 270 mm could pay for itself within a year; draught proof doors, windows, letterboxes and keyholes; keep doors closed; close the curtains at night. Insulate hot water pipes and tanks.

46 Fit double glazing – but choose wooden window frames not PVC: it is a most environmentally hostile plastic, it takes eight tonnes of crude oil to product one tonne, it's hard to recycle and can't be incinerated because it releases carcinogens – and it lasts only twenty years (wood can last a century)[14].

47 Low-energy light bulbs use a fifth of the energy of conventional bulbs and last up to ten times longer. If every household in the UK installed just three energy saving bulbs, we would save enough electricity each year to pay for all street lighting[15]!

48 When purchasing new appliances always look for the 'energy-efficient' logos. Invest in the most energy efficient.

49 Change to a "green" supplier of electricity; as consumers the choices we make are important, you are giving a clear and unambiguous signal to the market place

50 Have a shower instead of a bath – it's five times cheaper, using two-fifths of the water and heating needed for a bath[16].

51 Turning down thermostats one degree can save 10% of heating costs[16].

52 Put on a jumper if you feel cold rather than immediately turning up the thermostat

53 Turn off the lights when you leave a room (lighting accounts for 10-15% of your electricity bill)[18].

54 Keep your mobile phone longer – 15 million handsets are disposed of in the UK each year; that equates to 1500 tonnes of landfill, about the same as burying a World War Two destroyer. If you have to change take your old phone to a dealer who will recycle it or visit www.fonebak.org[19].

55 In its lifetime one tree absorbs the carbon dioxide emitted on a return flight to the South of France. Why not plant one[20]?

56 Avoid using machinery such as hedge trimmers for work that can be done manually – it'll help keep you fit as well!

57 Maintain equipment to keep it working efficiently.

58 For building or DIY jobs, always use the most environmentally sound materials, sourced locally. Use recycled materials (such as bricks) whenever possible.

59 If you're going to move house, think hard and long about how you can minimise travel and maximise the use of local resources. Also, think about how big a house you really need.

At Work

60 Encourage your organisation to adopt an environmental policy covering issues such as use of electricity, transport, purchase of stationery, etc. Such a policy can be used in selecting suppliers.

61 Reduce face-to-face meetings to necessary ones only, and look at alternatives like audio/video/internet conferencing.

62 Use a laptop rather than a desktop PC. Use a flat panel screen rather than a tube monitor – flat panels produce less heat and draw less power. Use an inkjet printer.

63 Send and receive faxes by email.

64 Print on both sides of the paper, reuse scrap paper

65 Use "green" stationery, i.e. stationary that has come from recycled paper, etc.

66 Refill ink cartridges rather than buying new.

67 Return computer consumables to the manufacturer for recycling.

68 Upgrade your computer with a new chip. That way you don't have to buy a new one. If you do have to dispose of one donate it to a charity or other collector (computers normally contain hazardous elements and shouldn't be dumped).

69 Keep a set of reusable plates, cutlery, glasses and cups for office parties and other use, rather than always getting disposable items.

70 Purchase Fair Trade products from the tea fund. Patronise local sandwich shops that use organic produce.

Waste and Pollution

71 Use real nappies and/or a nappy laundry service (the UK produces around 800,000 tons of nappy waste each year; for every £1 spent on disposables it costs the taxpayer 10p to dispose of them. It takes a disposable nappy five hundred years to break down in a landfill site. Compared to cloth nappies, disposables use 3.5 times the energy, 2.3 times the waste water, 8.3 times the raw, non-renewable material and up to thirty times the land for growing the raw materials – seven million trees are used in the UK for nappies every year[21].

72 Compost all vegetable waste – it saves the energy of having it carted off to a landfill site and, if you use if on your own garden, it saves on the artificial fertilisers (made from fossil fuels) and/or the destruction of priceless peat bog habitats.

73 Recycle everything you can. For example, recycling just one plastic bottle saves enough energy to power a 60W light bulb for six hours[22]. If your local council doesn't offer a doorstep service, find our where you nearest recycling centres are and what you can recycle there. Take a load for your neighbour as well. Remember every tonne of glass recycled saves over one tonne of raw materials such as sand and limestone; That means less quarrying, less damage to the countryside, less pollution and less energy[23].

74 Avoid disposable products in the first place, items such as disposable cameras, BBQs, plastic cups, paper plates, water bottles, nappies.

75 Use "green" detergents and household cleansers. Many of those we routinely use are a cocktail of abrasive, toxic and cumulative (even carcinogenic) chemicals, the long-term impact of which no-one knows[24].

76 Dispose of batteries, oils and chemicals at dedicated disposal sites (check with your local council).

77 Use eco-friendly paints that don't give off fumes and use water to clean brushes after use.

78 Buy recycled or second-hand products whenever possible – if they're in good condition it's a sign that they're durable.

79 Dispose of solvents carefully. If clean, use or pass on to someone who can use it. Allow very small dirty amounts to evaporate in open air (sprinkle on old rags to speed the process). For larger amounts see local phone directory for a waste disposal company.

80 Put a "No Junk Mail" sign on your letterbox. Register with the Mail Preference Service www.mpsonline.org.uk to stop 95% of junk mail through your letterbox.

81 Buy products that will last and/or can be repaired easily.

82 Use rechargeable batteries.

83 When you replace furniture or white goods don't just throw them away, donate them to a used furniture store (who will collect them). Details of local stores can be found on the internet.

84 When buying wood or paper products look for the FSC (Forest Stewardship Council) label – the only label that guarantees environmentally responsible and socially just forest management.

Saving Water

85 Invest in a rain butt and divert water from your roof downspout to use on your garden (some people say it's good for rinsing your hair and makes it softer!).

86 Install a water meter so you know how much water you are using.

87 Repair leaks. Fix dripping taps – they can fill the equivalent of a bath in the course of a day; what a waste particularly if it's hot water[25]!

88 Use water wisely. Turn off taps while brushing your teeth.

89 Install an utltra-low-flush toilet or use a "water-save cistern filler" – as much as a third of the water used in your home is flushed down the toilet[26].

90 Select native plants for your garden, you can save more than half the water normally required for outdoor plants.

91 Use a bucket when you wash your car; a hose pipe uses 300 litres of water on average, the equivalent of 33 buckets[27].

92 Using a sprinkler on your lawn can use as much water in one hour as a family of four uses in a day[28].

93 Encourage bio-diversity in your garden by creating "wilderness areas" to attract insects and small animals. Not cutting your lawn so close has the same effect and saves energy (it also stays greener longer as the soil retains moisture for longer)[29].

General

94 Begin to explore how big your Eco Footprint – the amount of land needed to feed you and provide the energy, water and materials your lifestyle requires – really is and how far you are above the two hectares per person set by Fair Earthshare. Put "Eco Footprinting" in your Search Engine and you will find a number of sites that that help you begin your journey. You may be surprised. The City of York, for example, has done an audit of the city's impact on the local and global environment and found it to be consuming over twice its fair share (www.york.ac.uk). Adopting some of these suggestions will allow you to reduce your carbon "bill".

95 Tell your friends and neighbours how important living more sustainably is. Share information.

96 Go and talk to your local MP, especially if he/she is a Minister.

97 Support local and national campaigns to promote sustainability. Donate money, it's always needed!

98 Volunteer. Get involved in local issues. Go on a march to express your opinions. Public demonstration still has an impact on government.

99 Report polluters to the appropriate authorities. What they're doing is a crime against us all.

100 Switch your account to an "ethically focused" bank.

101 Invest with a conscience. There are many financial advisers who specialist in ethical and sustainable investments.

And Finally

102 Take care of yourself with a good diet, exercise and a sense of mission to make the world more sustainable. Respect the planet and you will respect yourself.

References

Introduction

1   Paine, T. (1791), *Rights of Man*, Oxford University Press (1998), Oxford.

Chapter 1 - Setting the Scene

1   Brown, L. *A Myth Of Progress*, Resurgence, No 236, May/June 2006.

2   Cook, D. (2004), *The Natural Step: Towards A Sustainable Society*, Schumacher Briefings No. 11, Green Books, Totnes, p. 21.

3   Brundtland Commission (1987), *Report of the World Commission on Environment and Development, Report to the General Assembly of the United Nations.*

4   Commission on Global Governance (1995), *Our Global Neighbourhood.*

5   Anderson, A. and Cavanagh, J. (2000), *Report on the Top 200 Corporations*, Institute for Policy Studies.

6   Item on BBC News, 17 January 2005.

Chapter 2 - It's the Economy Stupid!

1   This phrase was made famous by political strategist James Carville, who hung it on a sign in Bill Clinton's Little Rock campaign office to keep everybody "on message" in the 1992 election.

2   *Dispatches*, "Supermarket Secrets", Channel 4 Television, 28 July and 1 August 2005.

3   *The Good Shopping Guide* (2002), The Ethical Marketing Group, London, p. 28

4   Farming Today, 11 June 2005, BBC Radio 4, This Week.

5   Rose, J. (2001), *Agricultural Crisis and Common Sense*, paper presented to an Academic Inn Dinner held at Swindon, 15 September 2001.

6   Ibid.

7   Dispatches, "Supermarket Secrets", Channel 4 Television, 28 July and 1 August 2005.

8   News Review, 17 July 2005, Sunday Times.

9   *Britain's Streets of Debt*, BBC1 Television, 5 June 2006.

10 For a more detailed discussion of usury and its role in the world economy see Greco, T. H. Jnr (2001), *Money: Understanding and Creating Alternatives to Legal Tender*, Chelsea Green, White River Junction, Vermont.

11 Ibid, p. 7.

12 *Britain's Streets of Debt*, BBC1 Television, 5 June 2006.

13 Von Weizsäcker E., Lovins A. B. and Lovins L. H. (2001), *Factor Four, Doubling Wealth; Halving Resource Use*, Earthscan, London. p. xxi.

14 Lietaer, B. (1998), *The Future of Money – From Global to Local Currencies*, Keynote speech delivered at the LETSLINK UK Complementary Currencies Conference, Portsmouth, 16 October 1998.

15 Report launched by Action Aid to mark the opening of the annual World Social forum on developing country issues; quoted in report by John Vidal, , Guardian, 27 January 2005.

16 Stiglitz, J. E. and Charlton, A. (2005), *Fair Trade For All*, Oxford University Press, Oxford.

Chapter 3 - Ideal or Bum Deal?

1   Paine, T. (1791), *Rights of Man*, Oxford University Press (1998), Oxford, p. 125.

2   TUC Report (2005), *Bowler Hats and Bureaucrats – Myths about the Public Sector Workforce*, p. 2 and 3.

3   De Gaulle in *"Les Mots du Général"*, 1962.

4   De Tocqueville, A. (1835), *Democracy in America*, Mentor Books (1956), New York, p. 303.

5   See Naylor, T. H. (2005), *The Swiss Model*, Second Vermont Republic, www.vermontrepublic.org.

6   Rankin, A., *"Punch & Judy Politics"*, The Ecologist, October 2004

(see also *Politics of the Forked Tongue* - 2002 - New European Publications, London).

7   Sale, K. *Things Fall Apart, Ready or Not,* Adbusters, January 2006.

8   Campbell, T. *Leadership in Creating Sustainable Cities: Lessons from a Global Practice,* paper delivered to the Sustainable Communities Summit, Manchester, UK, 31 January – 2 February 2005.

9   Swift, R. *Welcome to Squatter Town,* New Internationalist, January/February 2006.

10 Campbell, T. *Leadership in Creating Sustainable Cities: Lessons from a Global Practice,* paper delivered to the Sustainable Communities Summit, Manchester, UK, 31 January – 2 February 2005.

Chapter 4 - No Such Thing as Society?

1   Margaret Thatcher, talking to Women's Own magazine, 31 October 1987.

2   See, for example, Kapuscinski, R. (2002), *The Shadow of the Sun: My African Life,* Penguin Books, London.

3   Gaskell, E. (1855), *North and South,* Oxford World's Classics (1998), Oxford.

4   Booth, C (1889), *Life and labour of the People in London,* The Charles Booth Collection, (1988).

5   *NHS Crisis,* 18 January 2006, Independent.

6   *The UK Voluntary Sector Almanac 2006: the State of the Sector,* www.ncvo-vol.org.uk.

7   Dickens, C. (1853), *Bleak House,* Chapman & Hall, London.

8   Chan, T. W. and Halpin, B. (2001), *Divorce in the UK,* www.sociology.ox.ac.uk.

Chapter 5 - The Seeds of Change

1   Gandhi, M. K. *Mohan-Mala: A Gandhian Rosary,* edited by Prabhu, R. K. Navajivan Publishing House, (1993).

2   Aristotle, (350 BCE), *Politics,* translated by Jowell, B. Dover Publications, (2000).

Chapter 6 - The WHY Question and The Human Scale

1   Schumacher, E. F. (1984), *A Guide for the Perplexed,* Abacus, London.

2   Kohr, L. (1957), *The Breakdown of Nations,* Routledge & Kegan Paul, London.

3   From the Guardian, quoted on *Cool Kids For A Cool Climate*, www.coolkidsforacoolclimate.com

4   *Our Energy Challenge – Securing Clean, Affordable Energy for the Long-term*, Energy Review, Consultation Document, Department of Trade and Industry, January 2006.

5   See Greco, T. H. Jnr (2001), *Money: Understanding and Creating Alternatives to Legal Tender*, Chelsea Green, White River Junction, Vermont.

6   Sale, K. (2000), *Dwellers In The Land: The Bioregional Vision*, University of Georgia Press, Athens, Georgia.

Chapter 7 - Exploring the HOW Question, or "What Can I Do?"

1   Hock, D. (1999), *Birth of the Chaordic Age*, Berrett-Koehler Publishers Inc., San Francisco, p. 192

2   Uglow, J. (2002), *The Lunar Men: The Friends Who Made the Future*, Faber & Faber Ltd, London.

3   Iona Community, *The Common Rule*, www.iona.org.uk.

4   Hock, D. (1999), *Birth of the Chaordic Age*, Berrett-Koehler Publishers Inc., San Francisco.

5   Scott Peck, M. (1994), *The Different Drum: A World Waiting to be Born, and Others*, Arrow Books, London.

6   The Institute of Cultural Affairs (ICA) is a global network of private, non-profit, non-governmental organisations. The UK group can be contacted at ICA:UK, PO Box 171, Manchester M15 5BE.

7   The Scarman Trust is a national charity committed to helping citizens bring about change in their community, in a way that they want. They fund and give practical assistance to hundreds of remarkable people with a "can do" attitude. Visit www.thescarmantrust.org.

8   See Action for Sustainable Living, www.afsl.org.uk.

9   See Greco, T. H. Jnr (2001), *Money: Understanding and Creating Alternatives to Legal Tender*, Chelsea Green, White River Junction, Vermont.

10   Put "alternative currencies" into your search engine. Visit www.letslinkuk.net or www.timebanks.co.uk.

11   Wright, C. (2004), *"Trusting In the Human Scale"*, in European Business Review, New European, Vol. 16, No. 4.

12   Mabey, R. (2005), *Nature Cure*, Chatto & Windus, London, p. 212.

13   Although firmly attributed to Margaret Mead, there is no record of when or where this was first said. It is likely that it came into public circulation through a newspaper report of something said informally and spontaneously.

Appendix 1 – The Challenges Outlined

1 Report by the Energy Saving Trust, quoted by Lean, G., Environmental Editor, Independent, 25 September 2002.

2 *Is Global Warming a Greater Threat than Terrorism?* BBC News, 31 July 2004.

3 *The Sixth Extinction*, National Geographic Magazine, February 1999.

4 *Dead in the Water: How we are Killing the Sea*, Townsend, M., 5 December 2004, Observer.

5 Ibid.

6 *Oceans fill up with Toxic Fish*, Sunday Times, 20 February 2005.

7 *Britain 'Four Meals away from Anarchy'*, Sunday Times, 10 October 2004.

8 Laszlo, E. (2002), *You Can Change the World*, Positive News Publishing, Clun, Shropshire, p. 18.

9 *Planet Under Pressure*, BBC TV.

10 Campbell, T., *Leadership in Creating Sustainable Cities: Lessons from a Global Practice*, paper delivered to the Sustainable Communities Summit, Manchester, UK, 31 January – 2 February 2005.

Appendix 2 – 102 Things YOU Can Do Right Now

1 Ellis, H. (2006), *Food Miles*, article on bbc.co.uk/food.

2 *Miles and Miles and Miles*, 10 May 2003, Guardian Unlimited.

3 Institute of Grocery Distribution, quoted in Local Works: Campaign for the Sustainable Communities Bill, Summer 2005.

4 Findings of a year long collaboration between Northumberland County Council and the New Economics Foundation using NEF's Local Multiplier 3 methodology, New Economics Foundation, 7 March 2005.

5 *Smart Shopping*, Durham County Council website, www.durham.gov.uk.

6 *Energywise Cook Book*, Energy 21, November 2003.

7 January 2006, Saturday Guardian.

8 *The Eco Footprint of York*, Stockholm Environmental Institute, York, August 2002.

9 Ibid.

10 Lane, B. M., *The Green Car Buyer's Guide*, Ecolane Limited, 2005

11 *Your Guide to Making Less Waste*, Lancashire County Council leaflet.

12 *Do Good, Feel Good*, Good Energy Newsletter, 2006

13 *Standby Britain*, 23 June 2005, Independent.

14 *Death by Plastic*, 1 March 2006, Evening Standard.

15 *Low Energy World*, Mail Order Catalogue promoted by the Energy Saving Trust, 2002.

16 *The Eco Footprint of York*, Stockholm Environmental Institute, York, August 2002.

17 Ibid.

18 *The Eco Footprint of York*, Stockholm Environmental Institute, York, August 2002.

19 *Change the World for a Fiver*, Short Books.

20 *Do Good, Feel Good*, Good Energy information sheet, 2006.

21 *Cloth Nappies – Why Bother?* Fact Sheet, Unicorn Grocery, Manchester.

22 *Stats and Facts: Recycling information*, Recycle Now, www.recyclenow.com/facts

23 *Every Little Bit Helps*, DETR leaflet, 1999.

24 *It's Clean, but is it Green*, 19 September 2005, Independent.

25 *The Eco Footprint of York*, Stockholm Environmental Institute, York, August 2002.

26 *Water*, Consumer Utility Services, www.cus.net/water/water.html.

27 *Your Guide to Making Less Waste*, Lancashire County Council leaflet.

28 Ibid.

29 Ibid.

Index

Lightning Source UK Ltd.
Milton Keynes UK
UKOW030158121012

200445UK00001B/9/A